THE CLOWN MINISTRY HANDBOOK

JANET LITHERLAND

MERIWETHER PUBLISHING LTD.
Colorado Springs, Colorado

Meriwether Publishing Ltd., Publisher
P.O. Box 7710
Colorado Springs, CO 80933

Editor: Arthur Zapel
Typesetting: Kathy Pijanowski
Cover & Design: Michelle Z. Gallardo
Photographers: Arthur Zapel and Ted Zapel

Printed in the United States of America
Fourth Edition

Library of Congress Cataloging-in-Publication Data

Litherland, Janet.
The clown ministry handbook : the original book of clown ministry basics with skits for service & worship / Janet Litherland.
p. cm.
Includes bibliographical references.
ISBN 0-916260-20-8
1. Clowns--Religious aspects--Christianity. 2. Drama in Christian education. 3. Christian drama, American. I. Title.
BV4235.C47L57 1990
246'.7--dc20 89-77405
CIP

*To Jerry,
whose presence and support
are always encouraging,
always uplifting.*

ACKNOWLEDGMENTS

The author and publisher wish to express deepest appreciation to the following individuals and organizations who generously shared their insight and experience, invaluable in the preparation of this book.

Clown ministers:

Tim Kehl
Ernie Liebig
Carol J. Phipps
Bill Pindar
Karen Heath
Mark Clayton
Floyd Shaffer
Tom Woodward
Philip Noble
David Ebel
Ken Gosselin
Randolph J. Christensen
Marcia Graham
Ruth Hansen
Barbara H. Vander Haar
Ellen A. Ludwig

Thomas H. Nankervis

Magic, Inc., of Chicago, Illinois

Rick Tippens and the Belmont Baptist Clown Ministry

Connie Geiss and The St. Margaret's Merry Clown Troupe

EDITOR'S NOTE TO READER:

We ventured to publish this first book on clown ministry because we believe that this activity will grow into another valuable expression of Christian celebration and outreach.

It is our hope that future editions of this book will be as current and supportive as we have tried to make this edition. So that we may achieve this, we ask that you write us about your ideas and provide us activity reports of your work in clown ministry.

This helpbook can continue to be the best available handbook if you will help keep us informed. Your letters will be directed to Janet Litherland, the author, and she will use the information in revising the text for each new edition. When requested, credits will be given to the source.

Thank you in advance for your interest and participation in making this the best possible book on clown ministry.

FOREWORD

When I first began to use the term *clown ministry* in the mid-60s, I did it only as a way to affirm to my congregation and friends a sense of Christian authenticity.

To my surprise, the term emerged in places all around the world, and is now an understandable (though often confused) term in almost every denomination of the Christian church.

Clown ministry was, for me, a personal Christian journey, a journey into servanthood and childlikeness. That others have wanted to learn more has been a constant source of awe and wonder for me.

People keep writing and asking for information. There seems to be a real hunger to grasp some of the sense of hope the clown brings to a world that often reflects only hopelessness.

I am happy that Janet Litherland took the plunge. Many have wanted and tried to put together a manual of some sort, but have floundered along the way, failing to interpret clowning as "ministry."

This book is filled with a wealth of information and detail. It is an extremely valuable resource for those who contemplate the possibility of a clown ministry in a church setting. This, as one of the first books on the subject, covers only the basics of clown ministry. It is not meant to be a theological treatise or a comprehensive report of a new kind of ministry. It is, instead, precisely what it ought to be — a book of basics for beginners.

As this new ministry grows, as I'm sure it will, I hope that Janet Litherland will continue with future editions in her clear, concise style to give more people a sense of the possibilities.

I am glad that Meriwether Publishing/Contemporary Drama Service was able to make this book possible.

— ***Floyd T. Shaffer***
Socataco

TABLE OF CONTENTS

Chapter 1:

IN THE BEGINNING

An overview of the activities of clowns throughout history

Top three photos at right show the group in attendance at a clown ministry workshop in Madison, Wisconsin. Bottom photo: an elegantly costumed clown at the Clown, Mime, Puppet and Dance Ministry Workshops in Chicago, Illinois

"In the beginning . . . " seems a good way to start a book; and for ministry, it is probably more appropriate than "Once upon a time." But unlike the myriad ministry books that begin with justification, this one will end with it.

Many church workers, when starting an exciting new ministry like drama or dance or orchestra . . . or *clowning* . . . feel a need to justify it *in the beginning*. We are deluged with scripture that holds up cornets, trumpets, cymbals, David's harp, Miriam's dancing and Isaiah's drama.

Clown ministry, too, is often justified with scripture such as I Corinthians 4:10: "We are fools for Christ's sake;" I Corinthians 1:27: "But God hath chosen the foolish things of the world to confound the wise;" and Psalm 100:2: "Serve the Lord with gladness." It is also justified by pointing to ancient paintings depicting Christ as a clown, or by revealing the humor of God, or by noting the modern perception of Christ's functioning as a clown — searching for reality in a surrealistic world — as in the rock musical, *Godspell,* and the film, *The Parable.*

But isn't the caboose pulling the engine? Justification for clown ministry (and all kinds of ministry) must necessarily come at the end. For it is found, after all, in the answer to one simple question: does it work?

This book is about clown ministry. So . . . In the beginning is the clown. Who is he?*

A clown stands before us. His shiny green shoes are too big. His white suit is covered with multicolored shapes and spots, and it is too big. His ears, wiggling under sprigs of orange hair, are too big. His eyebrows move up and down on his painted white face, and they are too big. And his smile, the bright red smile spreading from ear to ear, is much too big. This entire person, this *clown,* dares to be bigger than life, and we are in awe of him. He makes us smile.

Children of all ages have gathered on the street corner to watch his magic and share his joy, but one child, small and shy, stands away from the others. He pretends he isn't watching. Soon, the clown catches the child's eye and moves his fingers in a tiny wave; and, very slowly, the corners of the little fellow's mouth turn upward. For a few moments, the clown entertains with bits of magic and a few balloons. Then he makes funny faces, and the children giggle and make faces back at him. And the shy child giggles, too. That's all there is . . . Or is there more?

Let's follow this *clown* to his dressing room. Let's see what's under the grease paint.

**He* is used generically throughout this book to denote all people, both male and female.

As we watch, unobserved, the pockets are emptied of props, the baggy suit is exchanged for a work shirt and trousers, and the skull cap, with its tufts of hair, is placed lovingly on a wig stand. Cold cream is applied to the face, smearing the too-big clown features. The make-up is slowly removed with a soft tissue. Now, after a soap-and-water wash and a final towel-drying, the face that looks in the mirror is transformed. It is a different face, yet something in it, something elusive, reminds us of the clown. It has to do with essence — the man and the clown are different, yet they are the same.

He sees it, too, and as he looks in the mirror, he makes faces at himself. He crinkles his eyes, he lifts his brows, he expands and contracts his smile, and finally, he sticks out his tongue and snaps it back into his mouth.

We remember the children on the street corner, making faces, and we realize that it is impossible to ridicule the clown. It is impossible because he has beaten us to it. He has already ridiculed himself. Because of this, we laugh entirely without guilt, not only *at* him, but *with* him. He is an enabler — he has freed us from ourselves.

There is more to becoming a clown than make-up, wardrobe and a few tricks. Not even a course in clowning ensures a true clown. He develops from within, from an inner warmth and an intense desire to give pleasure, to make whole persons out of broken bits and pieces. Does this sound like ministry?

Whether on a stage, in a parade, on a street corner, in a circus, at a birthday party or on the front steps of a church, the clown is recognized universally as the symbol of happiness. He creates smiles; he creates laughter. He stands for *good.* He knows no strangers, offers only kindness; he has no prejudice, offers only understanding. He cares. Does this sound like ministry?

Clown ministry isn't just entertainment; nor is it preaching in costume. It is a means of touching souls, something most clowns somehow manage to do. Perhaps all clowns, whether or not they realize it, are involved in ministry.

Many who choose to be clowns have had rough beginnings or hard times in their lives. "Laugh, clown, laugh, though your heart is breaking" is the theme of Leoncavallo's opera, *Pagliacci,* and is often the theme of life. To those who smile through tears, the urge to clown grows out of the recollections of difficult periods, not from a need to hide or cover up, but from a need to share. These clowns say, "I've been there. I've hurt, too. I understand. I love."

Not all clowns, however, perform through suppressed tears. The great Felix Adler maintained that inner sadness was not essential to clowning; and Robert C. Benchley, who clowned in Barnum and Bailey's circus in 1917, claimed that all the clowns he knew were "exceptionally cheery people." Clowning may spring either from a joyous heart or from a saddened one. One never knows what lies beneath the mask. Clowning is very often a ministry to the clown as well as to those he touches, much the same as a choir is often a ministry to those who sing in it. In many cases, a singer needs the choir much more than the choir needs him. In clown ministry, most clowns, driven either by joy, by sadness or by a desire to minister, *need* to clown.

A bit of the clown exists in everyone — his innocence, his enthusiasm, his sensitivity, his curiosity, his childlike delight, his profound emotion or his bumbling ways. Because of this, mankind identifies with the clown, and the clown makes the most of this identification. He reflects life and he comments on it. Through his actions and reactions, we see ourselves and laugh, not so much at the ridiculous as at the *comment* on the ridiculous — the old comic put-down. Yet, with the clown, there is a difference. The stage comic puts his audience down and leaves them there. The clown puts down, too, but he always picks back up, usually to a higher or better level of existence. "Because life is so hard, we have to lift up humanity instead of putting humanity down," says Marcel Marceau in *Making the Invisible Visible*. A good clown clowns *with* his audience, not *at* or *to* them, and because he feels good about being a clown, he leaves his audience feeling *good,* or at least *hopeful,* about some aspect of their lives. He is a creature of redemption.

In the beginning, clowns were in the business of touching souls. One such clown appeared in the fourth century when Diocletian was emperor of Rome. This clown, named Philemon, was not only a "fool for Christ's sake," but also was crucified for Christ's sake. Diocletian, who rose to power as an army general, was determined to organize his empire into an autocracy. He was an awe-inspiring man who flaunted kingly trappings and demanded that the people surrender all power to him. One thing, however, stood in his way — the highly organized, rapidly growing Christian church. It diluted his power.

To destroy it, Diocletian took drastic steps: 1. the army and the imperial palace were rid of Christians; 2. church buildings were demolished; 3. sacred books were confiscated; 4. clergy were imprisoned; 5. church government was dissolved; 6. secret meetings for the purpose of religious worship were deemed punishable by death; and 7. all Christians were required to offer sacrifices to the emperor and his pagan gods. This, the sacrifice, was considered the final test.

Philemon, a piping and dancing clown, appeared one day at the altar of sacrifice wearing the garb of a Christian deacon. Pretending to be the deacon, he refused to make the required sacrifice. When, finally, he revealed his true identity, everyone laughed, including the judge, Arrian, who treated the situation as a joke because of Philemon's reputation as a jester. Arrian made it clear, however, that a sacrifice was still expected. But Philemon, the Christian, was not joking. As himself, he again refused, and was sentenced to die. Before his execution, Philemon proclaimed, "The Christian's body may be riddled with wounds, whilst the soul within remains unhurt." Philemon, the clown, was executed and was greatly mourned.

In the 10th century, the church began to use dramatizations of Bible stories to teach the masses, most of whom could not read. Broad, exaggerated gestures, like those of the clown, were used, because they could be easily seen and understood. These plays became popular entertainment as well as excellent teaching devices. Mystery plays dramatized stories of the Old and New Testament; miracle plays enacted the legends of the saints; and morality plays discussed the common man and his problems with good and evil. *Everyman,* a medieval masterpiece, is still performed today. The plays, it would seem, would have provided enough drama to satisfy the needs of the people. But one important thing was missing — humorous satire — and the people craved it. Yes, Christians do smile. They even laugh!

With the "Feast of Fools" in the Middle Ages, they laughed at themselves — so much, in fact, that they eventually got into trouble. Feast of Fools was a festival held on one of the feast days after Christmas by the lower clergy and congregations. It mocked the crowning of a bishop, and included singing, dancing and pranks.

At about the same time, fools were also enjoying privileges at court. The term *fool* in the Middle Ages included the physically deformed and the mentally handicapped, in addition to gifted entertainers. Court jesters, for the most part, fell into the latter category — they were very bright people playing the fool for amusement and advantage. As Feste, the clown in Shakespeare's *Twelfth Night,* says, "This fellow's wise enough to play the fool!" Kings loved the jesters' pranks and practical jokes. Buffoonery provided a certain amount of relief from the boredom and rigidity of royal lives, and it was well rewarded.

Court jesters, like the church jesters, also mocked their betters. Thus, the court jesters mocked the state and, like church jesters, got away with it for a long time. Beryl Hugill in *Bring on the Clowns* says, "The tradition of tolerating plain speaking from the jester may have originated in the primitive belief that fools and madmen were touched by divinity and that any indiscretion was either caused by ignorance or inspired by God."

All of this lasted for several hundred years, but continual mocking of church and state finally resulted in the banishing of satire. Feast of Fools was condemned and stopped by the church hierarchy, and the performers, the fools, drifted to carnivals.

Clowns, as we know them today, developed during the Renaissance and are descendants of Italy's *commedia dell'arte,* a term that implies "skilled professionals." The actors, using improvisational technique, played standard characters:

- **Harlequin** — a shrewd, witty simpleton with a talent for mimicry. His gimmick was tumbling, and he was very limber and entertaining. He was recognized by his black half-mask, his pointed hat, and the colorful diamond shapes on his costume. He often carried a stick.
- **Columbine** — Harlequin's beloved; a coquette.
- **Pierrot** — a personable, light-hearted trickster who was often an accomplished dancer. He dressed all in white and projected an image of romance. Pierrot also loved magic, and wasn't above making his audience cry. They were sympathetic tears, of course.
- **Pantaloon** — a serious clown, recognized by his baggy pants. He had a formidable temper and a nose for other people's business.
- **Scaramouch** — a classy, elaborately dressed fellow who was always on the delivering (never on the receiving!) end of jokes.

There were others, too. The influence of *commedia dell'arte* was greatly felt in France and in England, and it very probably influenced Shakespeare, who used clowns for "comic relief" in many of his plays, including *A Midsummer Night's Dream, As You Like It* and *King Lear*. Shakespeare and playwrights who followed discovered that *clowns attract audiences!*

Toward the end of the 18th century in Europe came Joseph "Joey" Grimaldi, a talking-singing clown. Though clowns disguised themselves from the beginning, Joey was the first to use whiteface, originating the clown look that we recognize and love today.

In America, the first clowns were circus clowns, often sent ahead of the circus with promotional material. Again, their function was to attract audiences. Under the big top, they worked as time-fillers, as tension-relievers between dangerous acts, and as distractors who kept the audience from watching scene changes. Here, they were a different kind of enabler. They made it possible for the audience to enjoy the show. Many still perform the same duties today, though their status level has risen considerably. In the old days, clowns were very lowly circus members, not always treated well. Today's circus clowns are often skilled in areas other than clowning. They may be medics, mechanics, rigging experts or other kinds of technicians. Above all, they are artists, taking pride in their profession.

"All the world loves a clown." True enough, but — believe it or not — by the early 1970s, the beloved clown was nearly an endangered species! One culprit has been television. As a stiff competitor,

TV significantly reduced the number of traveling shows, resulting, sadly, in a reduced number of working clowns. The high cost of circus maintenance has been another factor. In most cases, circuses do not qualify for government support, as others of the performing arts do. To survive, many small units (as did large ones before them) merged to become three-ring, virtually eliminating the one-ring show. Many good circus clowns have been discouraged by this "bigness," because it has destroyed, for the most part, opportunity for intimate clowning, very important to the clown's art.

Despite this trend, more clowns are born every day. Nurturing is coming from clown colleges, clown organizations, clown workshops and clown newsletters, and by way of encouragement and recognition — the first week in August each year has been established as National Clown Week. Awareness of and interest in this mystical, magical, wonderful creature — the *clown* — is sprouting and stretching anew throughout the world. In Japan, where there is great respect for this bigger-than-life fellow, he is called "intangible cultural treasure." He is most certainly something to be treasured by all of us.

Into what coffers, then, will our treasures go, if, indeed, their places of work are diminishing? Where will the true clown go to touch souls? Be it coincidental, providential or a sign of the times, the most obvious arena for soul-touching — the church — is once again opening its doors to the clown, the "fool for Christ's sake." This time around, church clowning is called "clown ministry," and encompasses much more than the mirthful mockery of medieval days. Individual clowns and clown groups spanning all ages are successfully carrying the message of Christ to places where ordinary mortals either cannot go or would not be effective.

The method of delivery is certainly unique. It is perhaps even troubling to some, to those who watch from a distance, not understanding the heart of the clown.

Chapter 2:

BUT THE GREATEST OF THESE IS LOVE

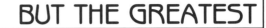

How clowns demonstrate devotion to God by their services and actions

Top left photo: Care and Bill Grey, a man-and-wife mime team. Top right: Randall Bane and mime student; middle right: workshop clowns in Madison; lower right: Randall Bane (Obie Good)

We have seen the clown as a symbol of happiness or joy. Yes, he's the funny fellow with the funny face, funny clothes and funny tricks, but the clown is more than just funny — much more. It is this *more that makes him a viable tool for ministry.*

FAITH

A clown is asexual, interracial and ageless. He can touch, at one time, all ages, all intellects, all strata of society, the living and the dying. Instant communication. He encompasses all human emotion and expresses it in a big, exaggerated way, showing his beloved audience that they might "let it all out," too, and feel better for it. In this way, he is a healer. By disclosing his own weakness, he risks himself, knowing not whether he will be praised or plagued, cheered or heckled. He is vulnerable to his audience, and he can be trusted.

Everyone has a "space," an area around him that is his alone. For most Americans, this is about two feet of personal space into which nobody steps uninvited. Example: two people cannot talk comfortably if they are standing too close together. Picture a crowded elevator and notice how the eyes shift downward or upward, never to the person standing close beside. This is because personal space has been invaded. Picture, now, a supermarket check-out line. People look at one another and sometimes even converse, because they are separated by grocery carts. Their space is intact and they are comfortable with it. More space, of course, is needed for strangers; less for lovers.

The clown knows about, and respects, personal space. With extreme sensitivity, he approaches the boundary, knowing instinctively when to stop. He clowns, then backs away, leaving the matter of space in his audience's hands. *They* decide whether to trust, to share their space. They may choose a handshake or a hug, or they, too, may back off. Either way, ministry has already taken place — something was offered and will be remembered.

Joy, faith, hope or love cannot be forced upon other persons. Children are sometimes afraid of clowns, and there are some other types of folks who just don't want to be bothered. Thus, these elements are presented so that persons may discover (or at least *believe* that they are discovering) for themselves. The fun is in the finding — the anticipation. In cases involving frightened children, the clown often aids them in discovery by acting as if he, too, is afraid. He takes fear upon himself and becomes the mirror, the echo, the means of release. The caring clown waits . . . and allows the children to come to him.

The clown minister has faith in God, humanity and himself. He conveys this great *faith* in some measure to every soul he touches. By presenting faith and offering trust, he shows that he is willing to share the trust of others. He offers a place to "Cast Thy Burden."

A girl sitting on a park bench is weeping. A clown (non-speaking) enters and shows concern. In pantomime and with humorous gags, he tries to cheer her, but to no avail. Finally, the clown removes his hat and weeps large clown tears into it.

"Is that supposed to be funny?" asks the girl. "Well, it's not! Nothing is funny!"

She reaches into her bag and, one by one, pulls out papers reading Love, Failure, Death *and* Divorce, *and angrily comments on how each has affected her life, bringing her to despair and desolation. " . . . And my parents told me this morning that they are getting a divorce," she finishes.*

Crumpling the Divorce *paper, she shoves it into the clown's hat, shouting, "Put that in your hat!" She then crumples the others,* Death, Failure *and* Love, *into his hat and bursts into new tears.*

At this point, the clown truly weeps. After a few moments, the girl looks at him in bewilderment and, hesitating, asks, "Why are you crying?"

He reaches into the hat and sifts her crumpled papers through his fingers.

"My problems?" she asks. "You're crying for my *problems?"*

The skit ends with the girl being touched by faith and offered a ray of hope. (Source: *The Clown As Minister I.* See Resources.)

Notice that the clown never intruded on the girl's space. He waited until she moved into his. He was her mirror, her echo.

"At our first clown rehearsal, we wondered what place a clown troupe had in a church. The silence that followed the first reading of 'Cast Thy Burden' explained it," says a young clown from the Southeast.

HOPE

Tim Kehl, a United Church of Christ pastor who has performed throughout the country as "Timbo, the Magic Clown," sees the clown not only as a symbol of joy, but as a symbol of hope. In an article in *Shoddy Pad,* a manual produced by the Office of Communications Education of United Methodist Communications, Mr. Kehl says,

"One of the endearing features of clown humor is that the clown refuses to accept the limits of the possible." The clown tries to ride a bicycle with wobbly wheels, walk a tightrope that isn't tight, or do any number of other "impossible" things. American clown Emmett Kelly fought against hopeless odds as he tried to sweep beams of light into a dustpan. Swiss clown Grock, an accomplished musician, would sit on a piano bench, and finding the piano too far away, would struggle to push the piano closer to the bench.

The clown fails and fails, but he continues to try. Somehow, sometime, he does succeed, much to the audience's delight. If that bumble bug — that clown — can do it, anyone can! He dares to make dreams come true. He gives us *hope.*

Mr. Kehl parallels this to obstacles, frustrations and eventual victory of the Christian life. "The resurrection of Jesus," he says, "is the supreme example of God's refusal to accept the limits of the possible." God, too, gives us reason to hope.

In the clown, there is always hope. It is seen through the lowly props he uses and his ability to transform them — a belt becomes a jump rope, a cooking pot becomes a hat, and colorful scarves become "fire" as the clown waves them in the air. Hope is seen in the smiles he awakens in persons who have had nothing to smile about for a very long time. The clown is a mediator. He understands something of life and the human condition, and he holds out *hope*. Even on his white face, the symbol of death, he has painted the colors of life!

LOVE

What is the ultimate expression of love? A life given for another. God, in sending his son to die for mankind, expressed the ultimate in love.

Love involves others. It is seen and experienced through relationships and attitudes; yet, there always comes a time when love must be put into action. Jesus, while on earth, expressed love through service. "I am among you as he that serveth," he said. He was involved.

As a symbol of *love,* the clown dies daily. Within his clown identity, he assumes a new self, ready and willing to be adored and humiliated over and over again. When he gives, he gives his whole self; when he shares, he shares all he has; and when he cares, it is with every fiber of his being. The clown is a servant figure. He has something to teach us of God and of the Christian ethic.

The clown knows that sometimes we have trouble loving others. Often, it is because we don't love ourselves. We don't understand the paradox of why and how we move in opposite directions at the same time. Even Paul the Apostle had trouble with this: "For I do not do the good I want, but the evil I do not want is what I do." (Romans 7:19 RSV) Is it selfish to love oneself? Not really. We are part of God's creation. He loves us. Shouldn't we love, or at least respect, what God loves? Are we not bound to make ourselves lovable and respectable? Through a shared love and with an exaggerated fullness, the clown enlightens us to the beauty and validity of the deep contrasts that make us what we are: death/life, bitter/sweet, selfishness/openness, joy/sorrow, fear/trust, dark/light, anger/remorse. By accepting contrasts as real and natural, we are better able to accept and respect ourselves. This frees us to love.

Through love, the clown helps us, also, to "die" a little, so that our lives may be filled with better things. There is a lot of love in the world, but too few are able to express it, particularly the "no strings attached" kind of love.

> ***"Love so amazing, so divine***
> ***Demands my soul, my life, my all."*** *

This is not to say that the clown is all seriousness. The opposite is true. It is through the vehicle of *laughter* that he functions, and it is through laughter, as necessary to life as breath itself, that we are able to reach out and grasp the brass rings he offers. The clown minister gives a little tug at rigid traditions, bending them just enough to put them in touch with humanity.

Strange, isn't it? The qualities that are the earmarks of a successful clown — faith, hope and love — seem to be the ingredients of a happy life. The clown embodies I Corinthians 13:13: "So faith, hope, love abide, these three: but the greatest of these is love." (RSV)

*Isaac Watts, "When I Survey the Wondrous Cross"

Chapter 3:

A MERRY HEART MAKETH A CHEERFUL COUNTENANCE

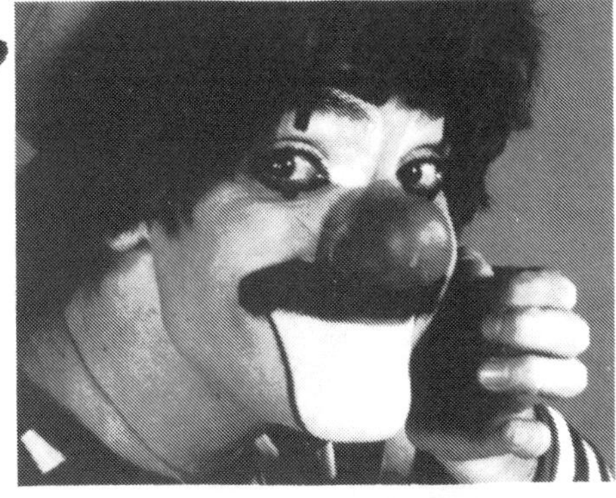

Costume and facial make-up of "pure" clown types listed and illustrated

Top left: Noel Strelak; top right: members of Main Stage Clown Troupe; middle right: Allan Tuttle; lower right: clowns in attendance at Clown, Mime and Dance Ministry Workshops in Chicago, Illinois

Everyone has a face — eyes, nose, mouth, chin, forehead and cheeks — arranged in the same pattern. Yet, except for identical siblings, none are alike, thanks to the genius of God. By our faces, we are recognized and known, and by our faces, we are distinguished from one another. Our similarities of feature unite us; our differences of feature prevent confusion.

Countenance also refers to the face, but it encompasses more than arrangement of features. It includes the expression of what is inside. Emotion. Being.

Ernie Liebig, a Texan and a professional Christian recreator known as "Happy, the Clown," says that a happy countenance is an asset "because it shows through make-up and rubs off on the audience." What a wonderful thought!

Make-up has always been part of clowning. Since ancient times, clowns have disguised themselves with masks, half-masks and dabs of color, evolving over the years into three basic or "pure" clown types, as follows.

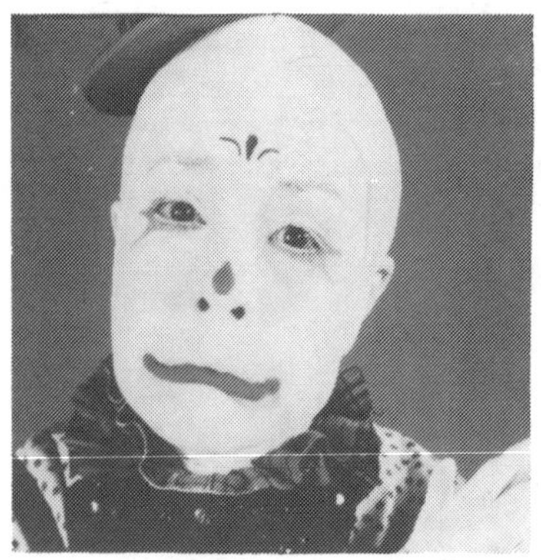

Neat

Grotesque

THE WHITEFACE

Descendant of Grimaldi's "Joey," the whiteface is king. He is smart, resourceful and playfully on top of each situation. His traditional clown suit, though colorful and loose, has some measure of elegance and symmetry. His face, ears and neck are all white, marked with red and black. He wears white gloves. There are two types of whiteface clowns:

Neat

- modest markings
- skullcap (no hair)
- small hat
- lightweight shoes

Grotesque

- bold markings
- sprouting hair
- funny nose
- oversized feet

THE AUGUSTE

Pronounced "oh-goost," this clown is the opposite of Whiteface. He is neither neat nor grotesque. His name comes from a 16th century German word meaning *peasant* or *common,* and that is exactly what he is — common, but greatly exaggerated. His wardrobe is bizarre — big checks, skinny stripes, loud colors. He has absolutely no taste! Nothing matches and nothing fits properly. His props are homemade and ill-constructed — they fall apart. He is on the receiving end of Whiteface's jokes, and, because nothing ever goes right for him, people love him and identify with him. He personifies the human condition. Auguste, despite his situation, is not a sad clown. A slapstick artist, he is a happy fellow and always manages, somehow, to recover.

Auguste

- flesh-tone make-up
- white around eyes and mouth
- exaggerated markings
- colorful clothing

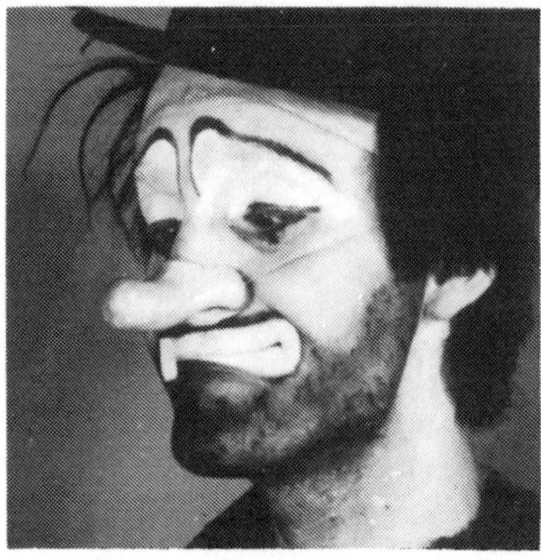

THE TRAMP

This fellow was originally called a "carpet clown." He was a circus clown who worked on the carpets — temporary floors laid in the tents to keep animals and artists from slipping. He was a laborer. He stayed near the action and created mood, often by imitating other clowns or by mocking the ringmaster. He also directed the audience's attention away from mistakes or accidents, and he cleaned up after the other performers.

Tramp is the lowliest of clowns. As Auguste is the butt of Whiteface's jokes, so Tramp is the victim of Auguste's antics. He wears discards and hand-me-downs, always ragged and shabby, but never dirty. His face is essentially his own, but his sad eyes and downward mouth set him apart from other clowns, as does his painted, seedy-looking beard.

Can a sad clown be funny? Of course he can — if he's truly a clown, he *has* to be! In the first place, everyone knows that he is joking. Secondly, part of the fun is in trying to cheer him up. People care about the melancholy Tramp and want to make him happy. America's version of this clown is the endearing Hobo.

Tramp

- upper half of face flesh-tone
- painted beard
- sad eyes and mouth (white accents)
- pink or red nose
- shabby clothing

From Whiteface, Auguste and Tramp, many variations and even mergings of types have been inspired, making, in many cases, identification of a favorite clown as a "type" nearly impossible. Though, as noted here, a pure clown type is asexual, interracial and ageless, many modern clowns are using their sexual, racial and age identities, such as a female clown's being easily identifiable as female.

Today's teen-agers tend to retreat from traditional clown faces and costumes, opting for a simpler make-up, colorful T-shirts and decorated jeans. Many see this not as a break with tradition, but as an enrichment — an input of fresh ideas. One influence on the current trend has been Oleg Popov, a soft-spoken clown of the Moscow Circus. Mr. Popov has developed for himself a costume and make-up that is more natural, less grotesque. His clown is beloved and very popular with the people. A clown, whatever his type or style, is still recognizable as a clown.

In the old days, when planning make-up and wardrobe, it was considered wrong to leave any skin uncovered because skin revealed the clown as human. Now, many clowns choose to show their humanity, perhaps by eliminating the traditional white gloves, by performing without shoes, or by leaving their arms bare, as do those who wear T-shirts. These clowns feel that their bit of humanness brings them a little closer to the people.

"But," you say, "I'm not going to be an individual clown minister. I'll be one of a group of clowns doing skits in church. Can't I just put on make-up and any old costume and not worry about what kind of clown I am?"

The answer is *no.* In the first place, clown ministry groups do much more than "skits in church," as we will see in Chapter 6. In every case, there is an opportunity for one-on-one — individual clowning — particularly in nursing homes and day care centers, where there are tremendous needs for personal soul-touching.

Secondly, each clown must develop (and come to understand) his own clown person. Each has his own face, his own costume, his own technique and his own special way of offering faith, hope and love to others. By tradition and out of respect, established clown faces, such as those of Emmett Kelly, Lou Jacobs or Red Skelton, are never copied line for line. They carry a sort of "moral copyright." Gags, however, are snatched, embellished and performed again and again.

MAKE-UP

The clown face should be designed (or discovered!) within a person's own face, using natural lines and expressions to suggest where the exaggerations should be added. A person with very expressive eyes may choose large eyebrows to enhance them; prominent cheekbones may call for big red dots or stars. Make-up should *reveal* the face, not hide it.

Rarely does a beginner get his face right the first time. The face, in fact, may go through a period of subtle changes as the clown person develops and matures. The face of a professional circus clown,

Bobby Kay, went through several changes over several years before it was "right." Head-to-foot snapshots, studied for detail, could help the new clown develop his identity. Sketching faces on paper, using crayons and other art aids, could also be helpful.

Within each clown type, the *kind* or *style* — fancy, dopey, wild pretty, etc. — will determine the make-up. Choose a beginning: dopey Whiteface? fancy Tramp? pretty Auguste? wild Auguste? pretty Whiteface? dopey Tramp?

You will need:

- tissue
- soft towel (for clean hands)
- cold cream or baby oil
- Witch Hazel (optional)
- grease paint — clown white
- grease paint — flesh (for Auguste and Tramp)
- grease paint — black (for Tramp; optional)
- talcum powder
- powder puff or white sock
- shaving brush
- lining sticks — red, black
- lining sticks — blue, yellow (optional for Auguste)
- damp sponges

(See Resources for places to obtain materials.)

Spread your materials on a table. Place the mirror in front of you and *sit down* — you'll be there awhile! In the beginning, plan on a full hour. If you hurry the make-up, your face will show it. Remember: make-up goes *on,* not *in,* the skin.

Application:

- Secure hair away from face. (Women: remove street make-up.)

- Either apply cold cream to entire face and wipe it all off, or pat Witch Hazel onto face. This is for protection and easier application of make-up.

- Spread a *thin* coat of white or flesh grease paint on entire face. (Tramp uses flesh only on upper half, stopping at beard line. His black beard is daubed on either with liner or a coarse sponge dipped in black grease paint. A little red may be used between the flesh and the black. Blend these colors so that there are no distinct edges.)

- Pat face with fingers to remove streaks. *Hold still* until powdered (next step) to keep wrinkle lines from forming in make-up.

- Powder heavily over make-up, using puff or powder-filled

sock. This is very important. It "sets" the face so that it will not melt or run.

- Using shaving brush, brush away excess powder.
- With lining sticks, draw markings — mouth, nose, eyes and decorations.
- Repeat powdering and brushing process.
- Outline the markings; powder and brush.
- To make the colors stand out, gently blot entire face with damp sponge.

The illustrative charts at the end of this chapter may be used to guide individuals in make-up placement and facial design.

Floyd Shaffer, a clown minister of world renown, suggests, in his clown ministry workshops, using adhesive shelf paper to make patterns for large features. Cut the designs and stick them to the face before applying base make-up. Then, remove paper and fill in the colors, powdering and brushing as above. Funny noses can be painted on, or made from a cut-out ping pong ball fastened on with elastic, or sculptured of nose putty. Putty is fun, but it takes lots of practice.

"I wear glasses; I need them to see!" some say. By all means, wear them. You will certainly be more comfortable. Design the face around the glasses, enhancing the frame shape around the eyes. If money is available, a pair of oversized, colorful clown frames with prescription lenses could be the answer.

Clean-up:

- Spread a liberal amount of cold cream or baby oil over entire face, rubbing until make-up is loosened.
- Wipe clean with tissue.
- Repeat.
- Wash face with soap and water.
- Towel dry.

Now you have a clown face. Do *you* show through it? Is your heart merry, giving you a cheerful countenance?

IDEA CHART

EYES:

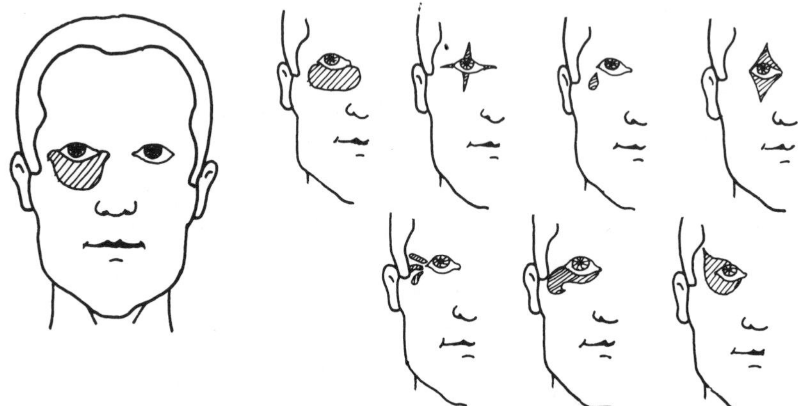

EYEBROWS:

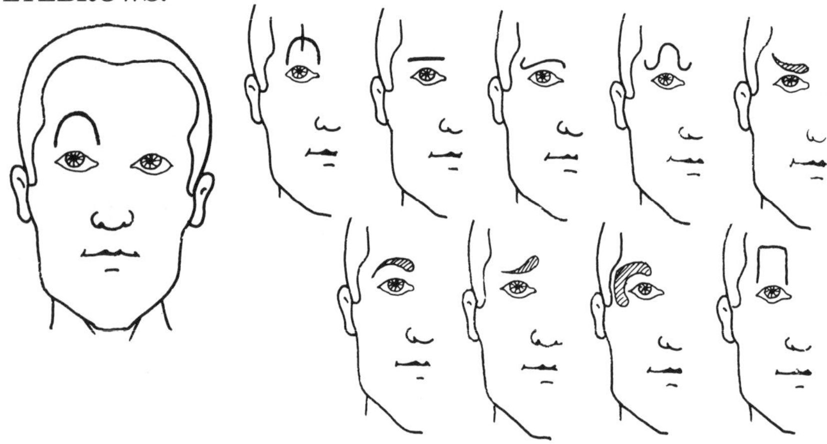

CHEEKS:

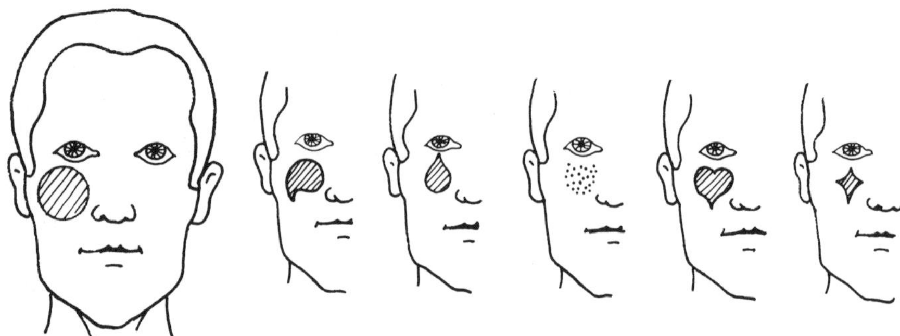

IDEA CHART

NOSES:

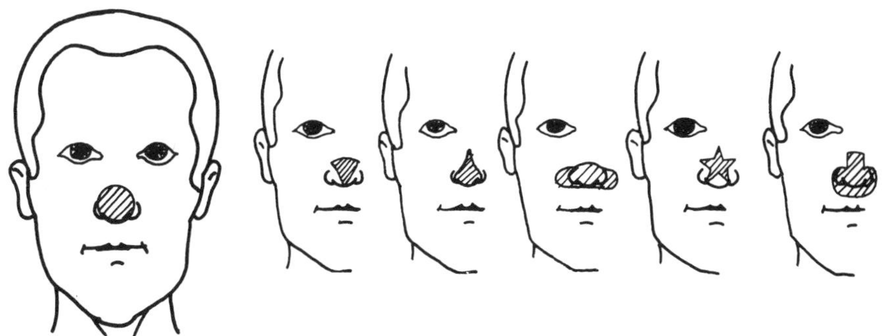

MOUTHS:

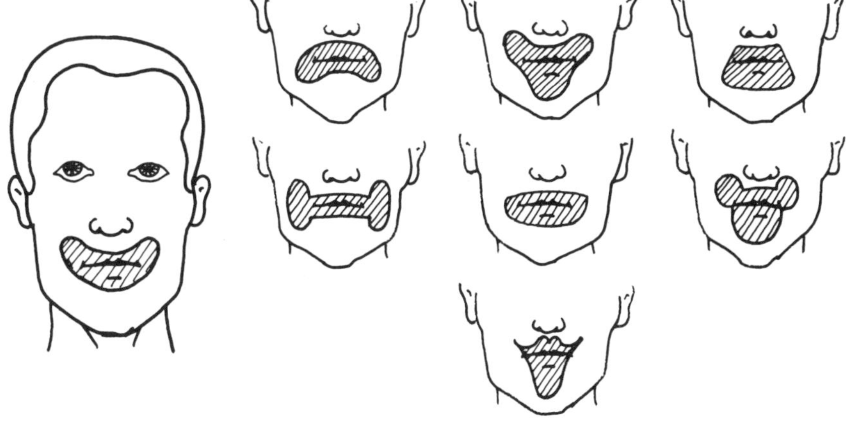

Clown Faces Using Various Idea Combinations:

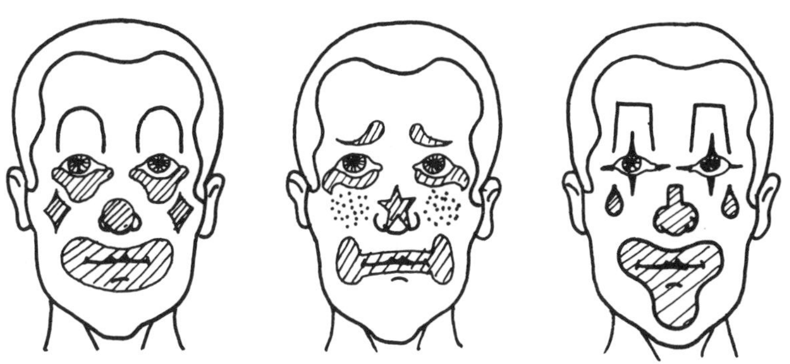

Chapter 4:

PUT ON THE NEW MAN

The need for a balance between what the clown looks like and what he is made of inside; stresses importance of wardrobe, props, techniques, name and feelings

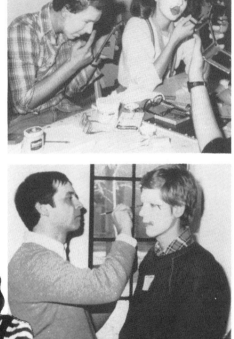

Lower left: Allan Tuttle; top right: clowns in training at Madison, Wisconsin, clown ministry workshop; middle right: Tim Kehl applying make-up to workshop student; lower right: workshop clown at Madison.

Tasteful and carefully planned make-up and wardrobe project a quality image. Seeing this image, the audience will expect (and get!) a quality clown.

We are "putting on the new man," or "becoming a new creature." This process refers to the whole clown person from the inside out. Many clown ministers relate this transformation to being "born anew in Christ." The clown person, therefore, takes on a new and sacred significance, and with it, a powerful responsibility. He is on his way toward genuine ministry.

WARDROBE

Clown costumes are not excessive. Flamboyant, zany, colorful, wacky, imaginative — yes, all of those things — but not superfluously so. Even Tramp does not wear *everything* he finds in the old trunk!

For Whiteface's basic clown suit, pajama patterns work well. They are roomy and comfortable. Polished cotton is showy and nice in prints, stripes, spots or solids. Velvet and satin create extra fancy costumes, but both tend to retain heat. If a clown is supposed to be "pretty," he needs frills, and additional decorations can be made of beads, sequins, feathers, appliqués, flowers — any number of things.

All costumes should be chosen with presentation in mind. Baggy pants would interfere with bicycle-riding; gloves might bother a juggler. Large shoes may be exchanged for smaller ones during routines in which oversized shoes would be a safety hazard.

Shoes can be painted or dyed. White tennis shoes are acceptable if they are kept white with shoe polish. Hats, suspenders, neckties, scarves, handkerchiefs and fake fur all make good accessories. Formal dress gloves (white) fit tightly and are used by many clowns as an "extension" to accentuate movement.

Want to stash some surprises? Pockets are great places — even on the legs. Need even more pockets? Cut openings in the sides of the costume and wear a carpenter's apron underneath, keeping props in the apron's many pockets.

Clowns discover delightful costumes in the backs of closets, in basements, in attics, at rummage sales and at thrift stores. Despite its origin, the clown's wardrobe is durable and *always* clean. Good grooming (including mouthwash and deodorant) is essential to the "quality" clown's image. His good grooming is also desirable for the sake of his audience!

PROPS

Props, or properties, are the gadgets the clown uses to enhance his act. To the beginner, a prop also serves as a "security blanket," something to cling to or turn to in a moment of crisis — something to do when one's mind is blank and one is at a loss as to what to do. In one-on-one clowning, a prop is necessary unless the clown is skilled in mime or dance. A prop can also become a focal point, an object of common ground between the clown and a reluctant audience. Examples:

- A child who is shy and unresponsive to the clown will often respond to a hand puppet operated by the clown.
- Props used as handouts – balloons, bubble gum, paper flowers – will usually break the ice.
- Children enjoy playing with soap bubbles blown by a clown.

About handouts: it is easy and self-defeating to let them get in the way of clowning. For instance, imagine bubble gum and a hundred children with their hands out. Use sparingly. Other kinds of handouts are used in worship and are more appropriately called "clown gifts." These gifts include paper hearts, crosses, nails (particularly during Holy Week), Bethlehem stars at Christmas and paper fish symbolizing "fishers of men." An imaginative clown might explore the idea of using replicas of the Chrismon symbols as gifts.

Unless the props are part of a gag or skit, one at a time is plenty. More would overtake the clown and overwhelm his audience, especially in close proximity. Deluxe mechanical props are available in specialty shops (hats that lift off the head, noses that light up, lapel flowers that squirt — *never at the audience,* only at other clowns), but often, the most interesting and most fun props are the homemade ones and the everyday objects that are used in different, creative ways. Here is a list to tickle the imagination:

- yo-yo
- kazoo
- small stilts
- broom
- feather duster
- bouquet
- pot or pan
- toy trumpet
- doll umbrella
- magnifying glass
- drum
- rubber ball
- alarm clock
- fly swatter
- toy telephone
- Rubik's cube
- bicycle horn
- whistle
- play blocks
- tape measure
- large feather
- jack-in-the-box
- ukelele
- string

- tricycle
- bubble pipe
- watering can
- jump rope
- catcher's mitt
- tambourine
- mirror
- fishing pole
- compass
- toy stethoscope
- butterfly net
- easel, palette and brush

Also:

- banners and scrolls
- chalk or crayon to draw pictures in the air
- big, phony camera
- telescope or binoculars with "eyes" on the ends (painted halves of ping pong balls)
- homemade oversized things:
    - knife, fork and spoon
    - wristwatch
    - pacifier
    - hammer
    - comb
    - scissors
    - back-scratcher
    - toothbrush
    - money
    - handkerchief
    - can opener
- homemade *under*sized things:
    - golf club
    - book
    - guitar
    - rake and hoe
    - suitcase
    - push mower
    - wheelbarrow
- small, concealed tape recorder that plays a song for clown to mouth the words (exaggerated, of course — opera, anyone?)

TECHNIQUE

Make-up, wardrobe, props. "Isn't that all a clown needs? Must he have talent, too?"

Talent is a scary word. It seems to imply a special, elusive commodity that God only bestows on a select few, and it scares away countless prospective teachers, leaders, workers and helpers in the church. Lack of it serves as an excuse. For most purposes, church workers need *technique* rather than talent, and this is something that is developed through study and practice. One is not born with technique. But there is good news: in ministry, a clown can be effective even if he hasn't yet achieved his full potential. The very fact of his insecurity, his vulnerability, makes him able to understand weakness in others, and, through this understanding, he can reach them, touch them where they hurt.

For the clown minister, technique is essential. It separates him from the clown who is content with make-up and costume, the clown whose character has no more depth than a department store mannequin. Through his acquired skills, the clown minister shows respect for his work and dedication to his special ministry. A clown in costume is just a clown; a juggler is just a juggler; but a clown who is a juggler is special. One such special person is Tom Woodward, an Episcopalian priest who is the founder and star of "Uncle Billy's Pocket Circus," a small street circus that has played across the country. A highly skilled juggler, Mr. Woodward has taught juggling to over 30,000 people. Juggling as a clown requires much more skill than juggling as a regular act.

Skills require time, patience, and most of all, practice. In addition to juggling, a clown might choose to learn mime, vocal mimicry, singing, dancing, tumbling, unicycling, balloon-twisting, pratfall, balancing, slapstick art, monologue or magic, to name a few. Carol J. Phipp's clown person, "Servo Servin," is a storytelling clown, utilizing one of the oldest known clown techniques. Technique doesn't have to be intricate and difficult. Juggling, for example, can be done with three, or even two, objects, relying on comedy moves to obtain the laughs. Unlike a magician who guards his technique, a clown often shows it. It's humorous.

The clown should also be skilled at exaggerated reaction and expression — a clown doesn't just cry; he *sobs*. He sees an object with more than his eyes; he sees it with his whole body. Raising shoulders, dropping shoulders, dragging steps, hand-clapping, hand-waving, jumping, knee-slapping, head-nodding, head-shaking, stomping and trembling all need to be practiced until they look effortless. Another funny bit of clown technique is to "take a set" — shorten the body by a few inches without appearing to have made a change.

Many established clowns feel that today's young people are too lazy and too impatient to work at perfecting the art of clowning. Let's hope that this is not true!

Wes McVicar in *Clown Act Omnibus* says, "The amateur clown

finds it difficult to realize that all action is *planned* action." Routines seem aimless and undirected, but they are carefully designed and executed. Nothing "just happens." Whether clowning alone or in groups, each clown has something specific to do and has rehearsed until it is part of him. *Clowns do not simply wander around.*

Silent clowns employ mime skills; speaking clowns often use altered voices or absurd pronunciations. Always, the clown's gags have purpose. Acrobatic clowns may fall, flip or sail across the stage, but something has caused this act, such as a smack with a broom or a bump with a bicycle. There is reason, however unjust, for the pie in the face.

Technical pointers:

- Exercise to keep the body in shape — essential for controlled flexibility.
- Choose a few good moves rather than many meaningless ones.
- Plan the main action, then divide it into smaller, precise actions.
- Practice in slow motion to perfect details, particularly a choreographed group scene, such as a slapstick "argument" or a "pile-up."
- Practice individual clowning in front of a mirror.

About audiences: the clown minister serves them in much the same way as the carpet clown serves the circus — relieving tension, enabling his audience to relax, and to obtain a new perspective.

Audiences need time to absorb routines, particularly those in pantomime. If the performance is hurried, they will often miss the joke; if the performance drags, they will lose interest. And they do not like being milked for laughs after a joke has ceased to be funny!

Hecklers? Heaven forbid! Yet, they do pop up occasionally and unexpectedly, most likely on street corners or in shopping centers. To retreat is to be wise. Quips or one-liners in retaliation could land the clown in trouble. Some people don't want to be bothered; thus, it is best to not do so.

In one-on-one clowning, the clown moves away as soon as he has obtained a response. He doesn't hang around, expecting applause.

In all clowning, the audience should be left with a good feeling.

NAME

"What's in a name?" wrote Shakespeare. "That we call a rose/ By any other name would smell as sweet."

Many famous clowns have used their own names — Joseph "Joey" Grimaldi, Dan Rice, Emmett Kelly, Lou Jacobs, Felix Adler — but the trend these days is to set the clown figure apart from the man beneath the make-up by giving him his own special name. The clown person then becomes a totally "new man." Even if he functions as a member of a group of clowns, he is still an individual. He has created his own face, his own costume, his own props, his own technique, and he will function better, more confidently, with a name to complete his unique identity.

Several clowns use their own first names, plus "the Clown," as in "Sandy, the Clown," "Walter, the Clown" or "Leslie, the Clown." Others choose names like "Happy," "Buffy" or "Bags." Some choose names that have special meaning. "Servo Servin" is the clown person of Carol J. Phipps, a Pennsylvania clown minister. The name means "I serve, serving." Carol chose it because, "I realized that I could most glorify my Lord by imitating he who was the greatest servant. I serve, serving and sharing with others."

Shakespeare was right — it is the essence that counts, not the name itself; but a name often helps us, and others, to touch that essence.

Chapter 5:

LET US EXHALT HIS NAME TOGETHER

Practical and spiritual suggestions for achieving and maintaining group organization while ministering

Right column: photos of events during the Madison, Wisconsin, clown ministry workshop; lower left, clockwise: Tim Crane, Frank Snyder and Jennifer McCabe

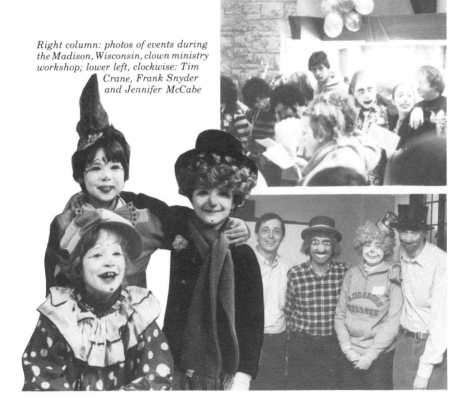

"Safety in numbers?" Sure. Why not? Most of us feel a little better when we know we're not the only "fool" around! But there are other, more important, reasons for forming clown *groups,* not the least of which is *strength.*

Grouping is the way we experience being "one body in Christ," sharing equally in the work toward a common goal. Each clown, with his uniqueness, plays a part in accomplishing the goal. Each clown is important. Together, individuals' power is magnified.

"OK," you say, "I understand about individual clowning, but what does a clown *group* do?"

Clown groups do individual clowning and also work individually within small groups. In large groups, they present dramatizations — often in pantomime — of a Bible study, a passage of scripture, a theological truth, a biblical personage or situation, or a theme such as friendship, poverty, honesty, courage, love or death. Such dramatizations can be extremely effective and are often poignant as well as entertaining.

ORGANIZATION

Every group needs a leader who structures the meetings and rehearsals, encourages achievement of goals, and generally keeps the peace — a tall order. In large churches, a staff member will often take responsibility. An active volunteer who has a deep interest in clowning would also be a good leader. Yet, the group also has the option of electing one of its own members. A word of caution, though: the leader's job is tough enough without the added responsibility of being a clown. One who doubles must be an extremely dedicated person, someone who is not burdened with a lot of other activities and commitments. The leader is ultimately responsible for planning and scheduling, though he may have help from elected officers who form an executive committee. Officers oversee committees on finance, advertising and production assignments.

A finance committee, headed by the treasurer, is essential to a smoothly operating group. Money will be needed for make-up, specialty items (unicycle, stilts, etc.), portable scenery, equipment repair, travel, publicity and emergencies. At first, the group may need to raise funds (more about that later), but after the clowns have proven themselves, money will very likely be allotted in the church budget for this ministry. The clown group's finance committee should consist of responsible persons who, along with the treasurer, are able to keep meticulous records.

If the group wants to expand beyond the bounds of its own church and community, it must advertise.

Publicity aids:

- word of mouth
- colorful posters
- banners
- brochure (can be a one-page flyer). Should be clearly printed and should include a photograph or drawing; references; complimentary quotes; a reprint from a press clipping (be sure to get the newspaper's permission if it's more than a sentence or two); a description of the group's special kind of ministry; indication of availability; business address and phone number. Mail to prospects — churches and organizations which might enjoy and benefit from the group's services.
- photographs (for newspaper coverage). Must be black and white glossy, at least 5" x 7".
- résumé (a listing of group's experience; include any individual clown whose own experience is significant)

Many groups include persons who do not serve as clowns, but who handle make-up, wardrobe and props, and assist in production. This works well, particularly for groups who need to involve many people as a ministry to those involved — something for everyone to do. But if the interest is in simplicity, speed and ease of execution, the group consists only of the clowns and their leader. Each clown is responsible for his own make-up, wardrobe and props, plus a committee assignment or production duty.

Some churches have found clown ministry an excellent way to involve persons with handicapping conditions, both as clowns and as production assistants. Clown minister Tom Woodward, mentioned earlier as founder of "Uncle Billy's Pocket Circus," has done extensive work with disabled as well as elderly clowns. One clown ministry group director reports that when his handicapped clown, complete with whiteface and baggy suit, pulls himself across the stage on crutches and begins making jokes, the audience is immediately moved to tears of joy.

A clown organization within a church meets regularly to practice not only skits, but also clowning technique. Meetings also include some theology and ethics — the things that definitely make clowning a ministry. In addition, meetings should include time for input — communication, sharing and compromise — as participants suffer together and rejoice together. The leader provides an agenda and enforces it so that precious time is not wasted. At the close of each meeting, he summarizes what has been accomplished and sets the date and time for the next meeting. The meeting immediately following a clown program should include a time for evaluating these questions:

- How do we *feel* about what we did?
- What were our strengths?
- What were our weaknesses?
- How can we improve?

Group etiquette:

- Be prompt.
- Be prepared to work.
- Be cooperative.
- Obey the director.
- Stay alert.
- Remain in character during performance.
- Give your best.
- Always clean up after rehearsal or performance. Leave the place exactly as you found it, or better.

IDEA BANK

- **In addition to regular meetings, a refresher mini-weekend is occasionally in order.** It not only strengthens the group spiritually and intensifies the performance power, but also serves to tie up loose ends by allowing time to do the little things that never seem to get done during the regular meetings. Here's how it works:

  The group goes away, if possible, to a camp or to the home of an accommodating friend in the country, or has a "lock-in" right in the fellowship hall of its own church. Each member takes a sleeping bag or bedroll for an overnight stay. Friday evening is for sharing and spiritual renewal, perhaps a reawakening to the significance of the clown through study or through the viewing of a film (see Resources). Saturday is for work — sharpening of skills, rehearsal and a planning session. Mini-weekend terminates on Saturday evening. Group members provide their own food and snacks. Often, they will engage a church organization or Sunday school class to provide one good meal on Saturday, covered dish-style.

- **Creative portable scenery** can be acquired by building several wooden boxes of various heights and painting them different colors. They become chairs, tables, walls, room corners, stools, rocks, risers, steps — anything that the imagination designs.

- **Fund-raising is a necessary evil** and is often a sore spot, particularly in churches with small memberships where the same people are drained over and over again, giving all they can give, and buying things they don't want or need. Here is an idea that worked extremely well in one Georgia church:

  Several types of instruction were offered — lessons in woodcarving, tennis, tole painting, dental care, economical shopping, basic music reading and even transactional analysis. (Others might be candle-making, quilting, canning and freezing, cake-decorating, carpentry or whatever talents are available for tapping.) "Experts" were then recruited to teach the courses, drawing from the congregation's own members and friends. A nominal fee was charged for each course over and above the cost of supplies. For instance, students in tole painting bought their own materials and paid $3 (total) for the instruction, which consisted of one lesson or workshop each week for six weeks. Sixteen people signed up for the course, bringing $48 to the project fund. All courses were similarly successful, each one reaching different people according to areas of interest. The only donation was teachers' time, and all who took part were well satisfied with what they had learned. There was an added bonus — fellowship. Many people found new friends through sharing a mutual interest.

  Other fund-raisers might include car-washing, lawn-raking and mowing, house-cleaning — anything where a needed *service*, rather than a product, is exchanged for a fee.

DETAILS, DETAILS, DETAILS!

In addition to make-up, wardrobe, personal props and technique, there are many things to consider when getting ready for a presentation. Here is a checklist:

- set props (furniture, backdrop — anything that remains in place)
- lighting
- sound effects and/or background music
- printed programs
- ushers
- invocation, benediction, offering
- prelude, postlude
- room decor

- handouts
- refreshments or reception following program
- nursery for children of workers and audience
- publicity
- chaperones (for traveling group of youth or children)

Success in any ministry depends upon each individual's faith, both in God and in the group's goals, and in his willingness to put faith into action.

The clown ministry group, or any group, will never be perfect. Like the individuals who comprise it, it is ever-changing, ever-growing.

Chapter 6:

GO YE INTO ALL THE WORLD

The "where" and "how" of clown ministry; places to go for outreach ministry, things to do and what to expect

Top left photo: hijinks at Madison, Wisconsin, clown ministry workshop; top right: Alan Tuttle; middle right: Floyd Shaffer (Socataco) conducting a worship service; lower right: Madison, Wisconsin, workshop clowns in action

All dressed up and no place to go? Poor clowns. Cheer up — the *world* is waiting!

There are many places where clown ministry can be effective. But first, a word about preparation — preparation of the audience, that is.

In outreach ministry (hospitals, libraries, nursing homes, etc.), advance arrangements must be made with persons in charge. Though clowns will undoubtedly be welcomed with open arms, courtesy deems that established schedules be respected and surprises forgone. Handouts also need clearance. There may be medical or other reasons that would prohibit their distribution.

To avoid a trip to the jailhouse, clowns who minister on street corners, in public parks or in shopping centers are wise to check first with the local police department; they should identify themselves and get permission. Not only is it appreciated, but it also separates responsible clown troupes from "some kinda nuts."

Outreach ministry is a good place to begin, and working in small groups of two or three is a good way to begin. There is some measure of security in having a friend to share the pleasures and responsibilities, not to mention the mistakes! Either before or after individual clowning, the clown group may elect to perform one or two skits (see Chapters 9 and 10).

Opportunities for outreach in clown ministry include the following:

- hospitals
- nursing homes
- retirement villages
- day care centers
- centers for the mentally handicapped
- camp sites
- street corners
- libraries
- schools
- parks
- prisons
- parades
- shopping plazas
- parties

For civic activities, clowns often serve as "come-ins," who entertain as the audience gathers. They may also function as "warm-ups," who work after the audience is in place, setting the mood for what is to come. Short skits and gags are in order here.

One must not think that the word *ministry* limits the clown's opportunities for outreach. It is not a deterrent. Remember, the clown minister reveals faith, hope and love, in unique ways. He doesn't necessarily do anything "religious." He doesn't preach or teach in the accepted sense of those words, nor does he distribute tracts. He is a clown and he functions as a clown. He is beloved. And he is welcome in nearly all situations.

Within the church structure, there are as many or more opportunities for clown ministry. Again, the audience — in this case, the congregation — needs preparation, particularly if they have never heard of clown ministry. They'll want to know: what *is* it? What is it *for?* What *good* is it?

During the Middle Ages, clowns appeared for a while within actual worship services, where they served as "divine interrupters." Their function was literally to raise the consciousness of the congregations by appearing suddenly, sometimes actually waking the sleeping folk. They encouraged earnest participation — better singing, more inspired reading, etc., then quickly disappeared. Even in this environment, they provided comic relief, and the services did improve after the interruption.

Some clown ministers function in much the same way today, though in a more subtle manner. Floyd Shaffer, a Lutheran pastor whose clown character, Socataco, is know throughout the world, believes that, ". . . When a clown steps inside of a liturgical celebration, he revives it for that day and he re-awakens within [the people] the mysteries of Christian worship." (from the filmstrip, *An Introduction to Clown Ministry)* He tells of one instance in his church when another pastor was preaching: at the time of the offering, Socataco, the clown, entered the sanctuary (without advance warning), following the ushers down the aisle. He carried a gift box, which he presented at the chancel. The other pastor acknowledged Socataco's gift and asked who it was for. Socataco gestured to the congregation, then opened the box in silence, revealing the elements of communion. He placed them upon the altar and exited. The other pastor, after a brief pause, asked the congregation, "I wonder if Socataco is trying to remind us that Holy Communion is a gift?" And the worshipers, re-awakened, proceeded with communion.

This type of "divine interrupter" clown ministry works very well if the congregation has respect for the clown and is used to seeing clowns in church. It is probably not the best way to "break in" clown ministry. A congregation can be wonderfully fertile ground, but it needs to be nourished in understanding the clown, just as the clown must grow in understanding of himself. The congregation learns gradually, with lots of tender loving care. Its members, especially those steeped in tradition, are not likely to accept or appreciate being shocked out of their pews.

So how does one "prepare" a congregation?

Let us suppose that a group (any age group) has decided that clowning is just the special ministry it has been seeking. The members have met together to study the clown — they know what he is about. They have developed individual clown personas and skills, have practiced technique, and have learned some group skits.

By this time, word will surely be out that something new and different is going on. A paragraph or two in the Sunday worship folder or in the church newsletter will confirm it. Carefully worded, it will also clarify what clowning can mean in terms of ministry. At the same time, the notice announces the launching of the clown group's outreach ministry — the new clowns will be working at the nursing home on Tuesday and at the day care center on Saturday, etc. The group continues to publicize its activities.

Next, an evening touted as "Get Acquainted with Clown Ministry" would be helpful. A family-night supper creates a friendly, embracing atmosphere in which the clowns can provide a program. Individual clowning begins during dessert, as the meal is coming to a close. Then, if the leader chooses, he may introduce the clowns individually and tell something about their outreach ministry, including personal experiences and anecdotes. One or two of the clowns may wish to tell what clowning means to them. Group skits are next, supplying the bulk of the program. They should be arranged from "light" to "heavy" — the funniest ones first, the more tender, touching ones last.

Another introductory program, perhaps for Sunday school classes or an evening worship service, could be the showing of a film such as *The Mark of the Clown, A Clown Is Born* or *That's Life* (see Resources).

A musical worship service might follow several weeks later on a Sunday night, with the clown group providing the "sermon" in the form of a dramatization, perhaps of a Bible story or of a theme such as *stewardship* or *mission.*

If Sunday night services are held regularly, clowns might take over the duties of worship leaders (not everyone at once) from time to time — song leader, scripture reader, ushers, etc. They might pronounce the benediction, using the very short skit, "A Benediction," from *The Clown As Minister I* (see Resources). It is important for each clown, whatever his assignment, to be well prepared, technically and spiritually, so that he adds to, not detracts from, worship. Worship is sacred.

When congregation and clowns begin to feel comfortable with one another, clowns may wish to start appearing in the morning worship service. (Clear it first with the pastor.) This service necessarily comes last as one for clowning because it is the most traditional means of worship — its forms have been preserved and jealously guarded for years. One or two clowns might break the ice by appearing in the pews, simply as worshipers. The clown as divine interrupter could then be introduced on a succeeding Sunday. It is just possible that, with sensitivity and celebration, the "same old service" will be expanded to new heights of experience.

Accomplished clown groups will want to try an entire service — a joyful, contemporary celebration, designed around an established order of worship. The group might also undertake a special service for a particular occasion such as Maundy Thursday evening or Mother's Day.

More opportunities for clown ministry within the church:

- programs (for meetings of youth, children or adults)
- Vacation Bible School
- children's sermons
- revivals
- camp meetings
- holiday celebrations
- homecoming
- entertainment (for banquets, parties and picnics)
- promotion (for advertising VBS, at fund-raisers, etc.)

Preparation of the congregation *is* important. It is important that congregants understand the clown as more than a "funny fellow." It is important that they relax their restraints enough to accept the sacredness of his unique ministry and to accept the faith, hope and love that he holds in his outstretched hands.

Bill Pindar, a Presbyterian pastor who is also a clown minister, tells of a Pennsylvania church that refused to admit two clown persons who arrived as worshipers one Sunday morning. The clowns were turned away at the door. "That would never happen in my church," says Mr. Pindar. "My people understand the clown."

This illustrates, vividly, Floyd Shaffer's idea that there are four stages in Christ's life and ministry. Note that they are *ascending* stages:

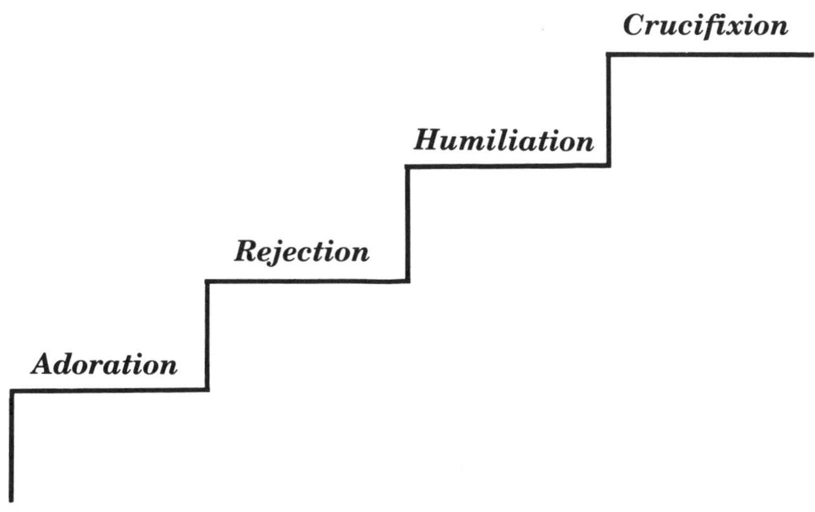

When Jesus said, "Come, take up the cross and follow me," he wasn't kidding. The true servant of Christ can only end up in one place — on the cross.

Whatever is done in the name of Christ and his ministry, whether it be drama or dance or orchestra . . . or *clowning,* it must be done with joy, sincerity and reverence, remembering that *glory* belongs to *God*. Glory does not belong to clowns. Clowns are merely mirrors. They reveal humanity and they reveal God.

Randall Bane, a noted Christian mime artist says, "General acceptance and effectiveness of performing arts ministry depends primarily upon the sincerity and devotion of the performer and the quality of the presentation."

There we go again — a "quality" clown. Not someone in whiteface who just wanders around, but a sincere and devoted minister.

Jesus said, "Come unto me." Then he said, "Go ye into all the world."

> ***"I heard the voice of the Lord saying, 'Whom shall I send, and who will go for us?' Then said I, 'Here am I; send me.'"*** *

*Isaiah 6:8

Chapter 7:

THINGS WHICH ARE NOT SEEN ARE ETERNAL

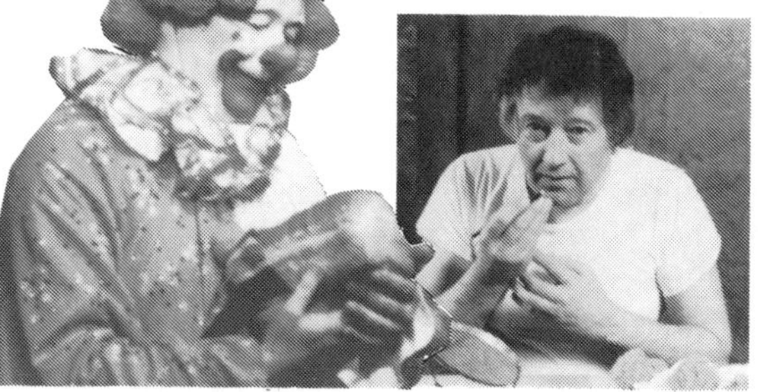

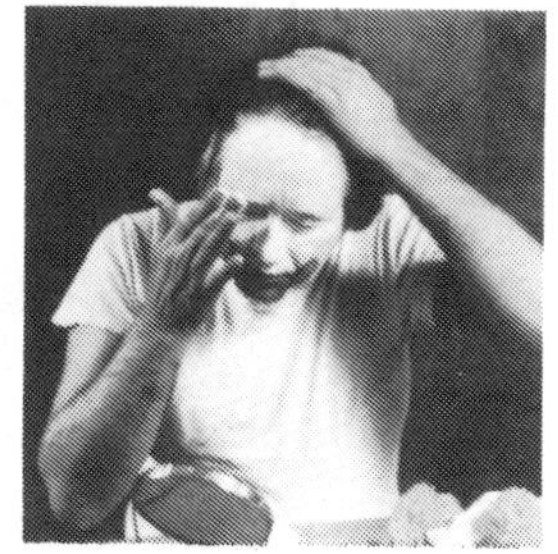

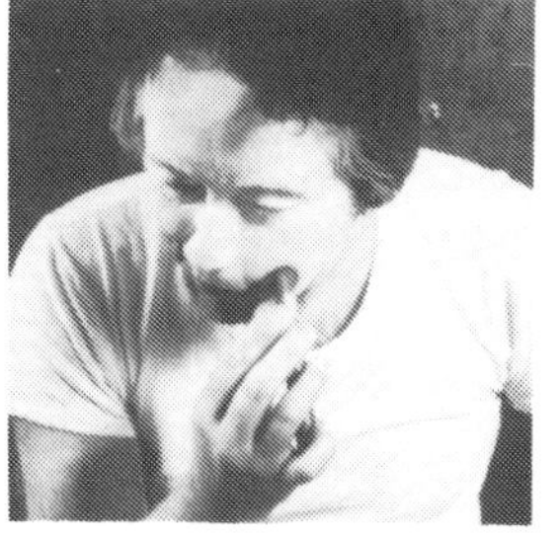

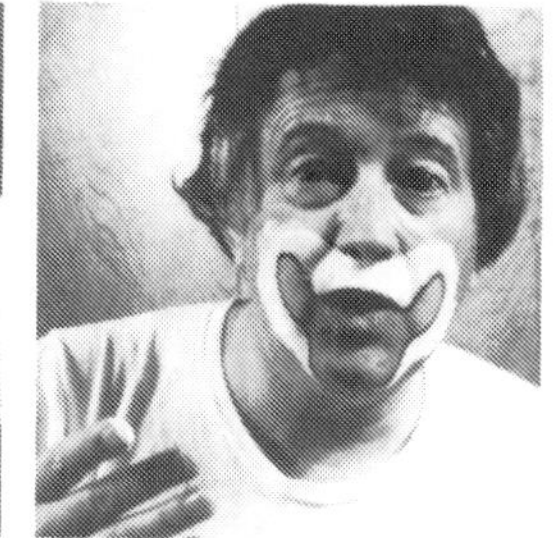

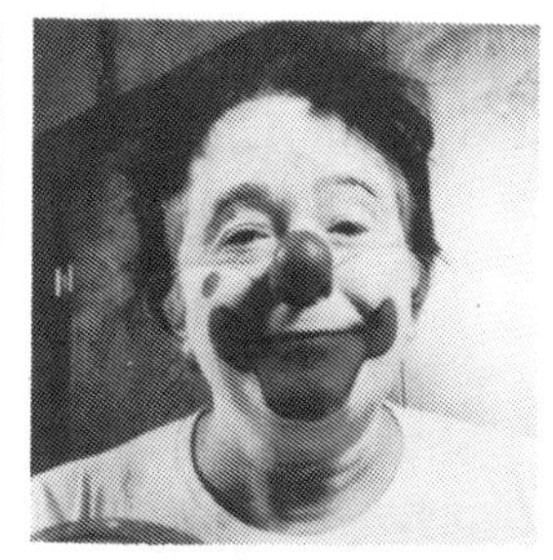

The relationship of God and man; how the clown can be the link between both; the importance of prayer

All photos: Floyd Shaffer (Socataco)

FREEDOM

The clown is like the wind, blowing where it wills:

> ***“You hear the sound of it, but you do not know whence it comes or whither it goes.”*** *

The clown is a bit of a mystery. His usefulness is not readily apparent, but we are aware of an elusive significance about him — sort of like an abstract painting. People rarely understand why he does what he does. It is later — often *much* later — that enlightenment comes, that special moment when we pause and finally say, “Ahh! . . . Now I understand!”

He is innocent, enthusiastic, childlike, curious, emotional, naïve, humane, sensitive and absent-minded — all things that delight us. He is also *free* to be all those things — something that confounds us.

From whence comes this freedom? From the clown himself. From the moment he “puts on the new man,” he is freed from the world of logic and restriction and is given permission to *confront* that world. His mask opens doors that do not open to ordinary mortals, and his big shoes step over thresholds built from all kinds of philosophical and cultural “gaps.” His white-gloved hands reach across fences barbed with doubt, greed, malice, jealousy, selfishness, despair and intolerance, all for the purpose of touching souls.

When a clown minister accepts his freedom, he also accepts responsibility, which is freedom’s balance. He is responsible to his Lord, to his church, to his community and to himself. Responsibility keeps life from becoming stale; it keeps a person strong. For the clown, there is structure in freedom, order in chaos, purpose in eccentricity. Because he walks where others cannot, he has, during any time of year, on any given day, at any moment, no matter how fleeting or silly it seems, the opportunity to plant the seeds of a “little Easter” — creation, sin, forgiveness, new life — within each soul he touches. He accepts the responsibility to make use of that opportunity.

This means he is constantly on his toes (especially *big* ones!), seeking ways of service with an attitude of commitment — not *outer,* but *inner.* The clown’s commitment is not limited to special times or places. He plucks flowers where he finds them, confronting and lifting up, allowing God to take it from there. He knows that God’s hands are stronger. Acknowledging that God is in charge keeps the clown humble. He is deeply aware both of the creator and of the fragile creation that is his clown person. He knows he hasn’t all the answers.

*John 3:8 RSV

"Responsibility? Commitment? There goes all my fun!"

Whoa, clown. Back up. Let's walk that way again. Commitment and responsibility are a part of freedom. Freedom comes to the clown as soon as he dons his mask. It is because of this that the clown is able to operate, and it is through *laughter* that he operates. He gives pleasure, ultimately making a difference in broken lives. He also earns a bonus: the pleasure he gives to others brings about a transformation within himself. Now that is *real fun!*

> ***"Where the spirit of the Lord is, there is freedom."*** *

PRAYER

Along with make-up, wardrobe, technique and responsibility, the clown minister must prepare spiritually for his adventure, which will be new and different each time he goes forth in the name of Christ. Because he serves as a bridge between God and mankind, he takes great care to see that the bridge remains strong. Daily devotions and communion with God are his greatest sources of strength. Prayer gives the clown minister *power* to touch souls in a special way and to put those souls in touch with God, who is the greatest soul-toucher of all.

Here are some good devotional scriptures to challenge the thought process in preparation for prayer (all King James version):

> ***"They that wait upon the Lord shall renew their strength; they shall mount up with wings as eagles; they shall run, and not be weary; and they shall walk and not faint."*** *

> ***"If any man be in Christ, he is a new creature: old things are passed away; behold, all things are become new."*** *

> ***"The things which are impossible with men are possible with God."*** *

> ***"Whatsoever things ye desire, when ye pray, believe that ye receive them, and ye shall have them."*** *

> ***"The kingdom of God is within you."*** *

> ***"For God hath not given us the spirit of fear; but of power, and of love, and of a sound mind."*** *

*The sources of the verses cited on this page are, in order: II Corinthians 3:17 (RSV), Isaiah 40:31, II Corinthians 5:17, Luke 18:27, Mark 11:24, Luke 17:21 and II Timothy 1:7.

"Be strong and of a good courage; be not afraid, neither be thou dismayed: for the Lord thy God is with thee whithersoever thou goest." *

"Eye hath not seen, nor ear heard, neither have entered into the heart of man, the things which God hath prepared for them that love him." *

"In him we live, and move, and have our being." *

"Peace I leave with you, my peace I give unto you: not as the world giveth, give I unto you. Let not your heart be troubled, neither let it be afraid." *

Prayer

Lord, make me an instrument of thy peace:
Where there is hatred, let me sow love;
Where there is injury, pardon;
Where there is doubt, faith;
Where there is despair, hope;
Where there is darkness, light;
Where there is sadness, joy.

O Divine Master, grant that I may not so much seek
To be consoled as to console,
To be understood as to understand,
To be loved as to love;
For it is in giving that we receive;
It is in pardoning that we are pardoned;
It is in dying that we are born to eternal life!

— St. Francis of Assisi

DOES IT WORK?

It is time for justification, if, indeed, it exists. In using the question *Does it work?* as the basis, we must reply to those who will argue that the end never justifies the means.

In this case, it does. *End* is defined as a closer relationship with God, and *means* as a ministry that accomplishes that end. In

*The sources of the verses (all King James version) cited on this page are, in order: Joshua 1:9, I Corinthians 2:9, Acts 17:28 and John 14:27.

any ministry, the tools used are just that — tools. Unless they enable a closer walk with God, they are useless. If the clown's ministry doesn't work, it is not valid, and no amount of historic rationale or supportive scripture will make it right. If it works . . . if it touches souls who might otherwise remain untouched, it is a valid, worthwhile ministry.

> *One day when the prophet Elijah was standing in the marketplace, a friend of his came up to him and asked, "Is there anybody in the multitude who will have a share in the World to Come?"*
>
> *Elijah looked about him, and with a sigh, he answered: "No."*
>
> *Then he looked about again and pointed to two men who had just entered the marketplace and were making their way through the crowds. "Those two will have a share in the World to Come."*
>
> *"What is their occupation, and what have they done to deserve it?" asked Elijah's friend.*
>
> *"They are clowns," Elijah replied, "and when they see people troubled in mind or heavy with sorrow, they make them laugh; and when they meet people who quarrel, they make peace between them"* *

Where will the true clown go to touch souls? Will he find a home within the church, involved in mission and outreach, doing *good?* Is the church a place for touching souls? Is the church a place for the clown?

Faith, hope, love, joy, freedom, responsibility, commitment, prayer and peace — these things are eternal. They are *the clown minister,* a clown who has chosen to be . . . *a clown of God!*

**The Talmud:* Moed-Taanith, 22a: *The Lore of the Old Testament,* by Joseph Gaer, Little, Brown and Company, Boston, 1951. © 1951 by Joseph Gaer.

Chapter 8:

CLOWN GAGS

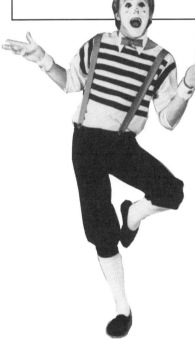

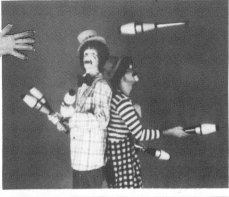

Suggestions to the clown for achieving rapport with audience, through laughter

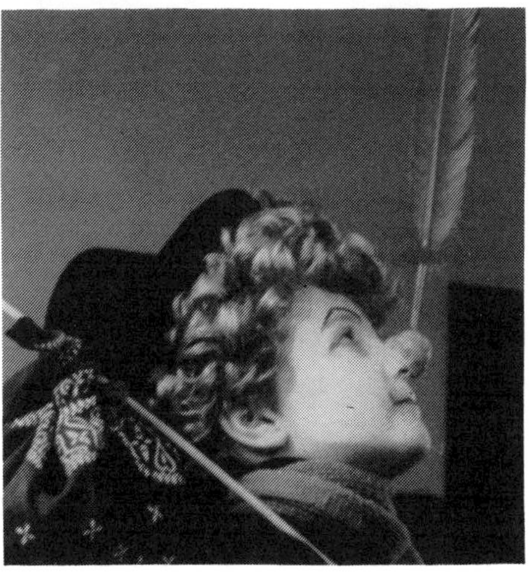

Top left: Bill Grey, mime; top right and center right: Main Stage clowns in action; lower right: kid clown, Frank Snyder

THE CLOWN "SHOWS ALL"

Ernie Kerns in *How to Be a Magic Clown, Vol. II,* says, "As a clown, you should always make the slip that shows you for the faker you are." Good advice. The audience loves catching the clown in his "mistakes."

- Using a fake barbell, a clown struggles and struggles to lift, but can't get more than a few inches off the ground. "The world's heaviest barbell," he brags. "No one can lift it." Enter next clown with juggling trick. "I need room," says second clown. "Move that barbell." Eager to see the juggling, first clown quickly lifts the barbell with one hand and tosses it to side of stage, unwittingly exposing it as fake. Immediately, he realizes his mistake and reacts with embarrassment.
- Juggling clown delivers his "new" act, accidently revealing that one or more of his objects is returning by means of a thin elastic band.
- Clown, with great difficulty, balances a straw on the end of his finger, only to reveal, as he takes his bow, that the straw is stuck to his finger. This effect can be achieved by using chewing gum or a less messy product called Plasti-Tak™, available in most variety stores. Plasti-Tak™ will stick to anything (except grease paint) and can be easily and safely removed.
- Clown twirls an open umbrella, keeping a rubber ball rolling on the outside. Actually, the ball is attached with strong thread to the tip of the umbrella. Audience discovers the fraud when clown closes the umbrella and walks off, ball dangling (idea from *How to Be a Magic Clown, Vol. I).*

JUST FOR FUN

- "Ladies and Gentlemen, I have been asked to announce that after Monday and Tuesday, there will follow Wednesday and Thursday."
- Clown with sketch pad and pencil elaborately sketches a member of the audience, holding out his thumb several times to gain perspective. Finished, he smiles and proudly turns his work around. He has sketched a huge thumb!
- Clown carries a spouted can clearly labeled *oil.* He uses it to "oil" his joints — elbows, knees, hips, etc. — showing audience how much better the joints work when oiled.
- Clown offers a long-stemmed flower to a lady in the audience. He holds it near the bloom, offering it to her by the stem. But

he has cut the stem, and when he walks away, the bloom remains in his hand, leaving the lady with only the stem.

- Clown tosses a small amount of confetti onto his audience, then proceeds, with his feather duster, to dust off those who want to be dusted. Children, especially, like this.
- Clown photographer poses his subject (another clown) for a formal portrait. He is fussy about the pose and stops several times to adjust and re-adjust the subject, who becomes increasingly exasperated. Finally, he snaps the picture, suddenly realizing that he forgot the film. He opens his camera to show that it is empty, and subject clown angrily chases him offstage.
- Two clowns try to crawl beneath a limbo rod. One always succeeds, but the other never does, because first clown keeps changing the position of the rod when second clown isn't looking — he's busy explaining to the audience that *this* time, he will do it. Second clown finally *jumps* the rod and exits, whistling. First clown follows, angrily waving rod in the air.
- Clown places long rope on ground in straight line. He makes an issue of getting it just right, then proceeds to walk across it as if it were a high wire, balancing himself with outstretched arms.
- Clown in long underwear carries suitcase and stepladder across stage, explaining to audience as he hurries along, "I lost my suit, so I'm taking my case to a higher court."

(The second, fourth, fifth and ninth ideas are adapted from *How to Be a Magic Clown, Vols. I & II.)*

Ideas to develop:

- a game show
- a beauty pageant
- ballet
- echo play
- hide and seek
- an awards ceremony
- a baseball game
- a drill team routine
- cowboys and Indians
- organ grinder and monkey
- creatures from outer space
- graduation
- cooking school
- bowling

Other sources of funny material:

- nursery rhymes
- children's books
- puppet plays
- proverbs and maxims

- legends
- stories
- poetry
- TV commercials
- songs
- comic strips

Chapter 9:

SCRIPTURE SKITS FOR CLOWN GROUPS

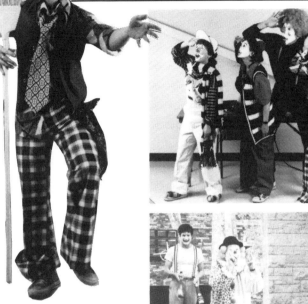

Includes five skits, each with several clown parts; skits with a message for Christian living

Top left: John Sideris; top right: Kristen Sideris, Rose Wanner, Art Zapel and John Sideris; middle right: Floyd Shaffer (Socataco); lower right: clown worship service, Madison, Wisconsin

Skit #1

Gideon's Army*

INSTRUCTIONS: Eleven clowns, each with a toy trumpet. Four of them also have a small fry pan and flashlight each. Eight or more people not in clown garb (ENEMY), each with a cardboard "sword." One narrator, seated on high stool at extreme Downstage Right. Clowns pantomime everything NARRATOR says.

(GIDEON, one of the clowns, enters Left and moves Center.)

NARRATOR: This is Gideon. *(Pauses while GIDEON blows his trumpet, regardless of quality of sound. Ten clowns hurry in from Left to behind GIDEON.)* **And this is his army.** *(Clowns blow horns.)* **Frightening, aren't they? They have been preparing for battle —** *(Clowns flex muscles and otherwise show off.)* **a *huge* battle with the Midianites.** *(Clowns demonstrate* huge.*)*

But along comes the Lord and says to Gideon, "There are too many of you to fight this battle. *(Clowns react — they count themselves; some pantomime a protest to God, out over the audience's heads.)* **Don't argue with me, Gideon. I know what I'm doing. Find out which of your men are afraid and send them home.** *(Three clowns admit their fear and, trembling, leave the stage.)* **Only three, Gideon? . . . There are still too many.** *(Clowns protest.)* **Gideon, come here.** *(GIDEON moves Downstage. Other clowns talk among themselves.)* **Take your men to the stream and ask them to drink. We will separate them by the way they drink.** *(GIDEON scratches his head in bewilderment.)* **Do as I say."**

. . . So Gideon took his men to the stream and bade them drink. Some cupped their hands and lapped water from them *(Three clowns)*; **others leaned over and drank directly from the stream** *(Four clowns)*. **When they were finished, God said, "I will take those who drank from**

*Performance rights for this skit are granted with the purchase of this book. No further permission is needed to adapt or integrate this skit within any performance situation for clown ministry. Excerpted from *Scripture Skits for a Troupe of Clowns* by Janet Litherland. Available from Contemporary Drama Service. See RESOURCES.

cupped hands. Send the others home." *(GIDEON reluctantly does as God says.)*

Why did God choose in this manner? Perhaps because those who cupped their hands would be more likely to keep a watchful eye toward the enemy.

"Now," says God to Gideon, "we will conquer the Midianites." *(GIDEON surveys his tiny army and shakes his head in dismay. Clowns stretch out on the floor for a rest.)* **That night, while his men were resting, Gideon overheard them discussing a dream, which they interpreted as a sign that Gideon's army, pathetic though it was, would defeat the enemy. Encouraged, Gideon roused his men, shouting, "With the Lord's help, we will conquer the Midianites!" He then checked their weapons,** *(Clowns pull out pans and flashlights to go with their trumpets.)* **and explained his plan.** *(Clowns exit Left. Enemies with swords enter Right and sit in a circle, Stage Right.)*

Just after dark, Gideon and his men crept up to the Midianite camp. *(Clowns enter Left and creep toward enemy.)* **Suddenly, they —** *(Clowns throw down their pans to make noise, blow their trumpets, and shine their lights at the enemies. The enemies, terrified, run around in a panic and finally exit, Right.)* **Gideon's men were delighted that the enemy had been so easily overcome.** *(Clowns show delight.)* **For that matter, so was Gideon, though he wasn't terribly surprised.** *(GIDEON shakes head.)* **He had learned, you see, to trust in God.** *(GIDEON salutes God as all exit.)*

Skit #2

The Needle's Eye*

INSTRUCTIONS: Two clowns. Clown 1 has large needle and a length of thread. Clown 2 has balloons tied around his waist. Clown 1 is seated, trying, unsuccessfully, to thread his needle.

CLOWN 2: *(Enters, watches for a while, then asks:)* **Why are you**

*Performance rights for this skit are granted with the purchase of this book. No further permission is needed to adapt or integrate this skit within any performance situation for clown ministry.

doing that?

CLOWN 1: No reason.

CLOWN 2: Why is the needle so big?

CLOWN 1: It's an old-timey one. Even so, it's pretty hard to figure how a camel could go through the eye.

CLOWN 2: Huh?

CLOWN 1: You know — "It's easier for a camel to go through a needle's eye than for a rich man to get into heaven," or something like that.

CLOWN 2: Aw, that's not even the same kind of needle's eye.

CLOWN 1: It's not?

CLOWN 2: No. The needle's eye was a little door within a city gate. *(He gestures.)* **A man could go through, but a camel with his big humps would have an awful time pushing and squeezing.**

CLOWN 1: *(Rises.)* **Show me.**

CLOWN 2: Well . . . *(He kneels, facing away from CLOWN 1.)* **If the door was this high,** *(Gestures.)* **and if these balloons were camel's humps, I wouldn't be able to get through.** *(He pantomimes struggling.)*

CLOWN 1: I can fix that. *(He pops the balloons with his needle.)* **Get the point?** *(He runs Offstage, with CLOWN 2 yelling and chasing him.)*

Skit #3

A Parable*

INSTRUCTIONS: Eight or more clowns. NARRATOR (a clown) reads the following story, eliminating directions in parentheses, as other clowns pantomime it in slapstick fashion.

NARRATOR: Once upon a time, a businessman was walking from *(Your town)* **to** *(A nearby town)***. His car had broken down, you see. He didn't really mind the walk; it was a**

*Performance rights for this skit are granted with the purchase of this book. No further permission is needed to adapt or integrate this skit within any performance situation for clown ministry. Excerpted from *Scripture Skits for a Troupe of Clowns* by Janet Litherland. Available from Contemporary Drama Service. See RESOURCES.

nice day and he was happy. But along came a motorcycle gang . . . *(Could be clowns on unicycles or bicycles with toy "stick" horses.)* **and, attracted by his important-looking briefcase, they decided to mug him. . . . They beat him . . .** *(With balloons or something equally harmless)* **They robbed him . . . and even took his wonderful new coat and hat, *varooming* off without so much as a backward look. Now it happened that a** *(Your denomination)* **preacher came along that way in his car** *(A scooter)*. **He looked at the poor, helpless soul in the ditch, and then looked at his watch** *(An oversized one)*. **He was almost late for the Women's Society chicken supper and, after all, he was expected to ask the blessing. "Ah, well," he thought, "this is a busy road. Someone else will help." Shrugging, he hurried on.**

A few moments later, another man came along. He could tell by the poor soul's face that they were members of the same club *(Compare clown faces.)*, **but it would be a shame to get all dirty trying to help a guy who was probably dead anyway.** *(Clown on ground tries to get his attention.)* **So he went on by, pretending he hadn't noticed.**

But then along came a man *(Wearing a backpack)* **from** *(A rival city)*. **He was walking, not because his car had broken down, but because he didn't own a car. He was dusty and perspiring, and, like the others, he, too, was in a hurry — he was meeting some of his friends for an evening of poker. Nevertheless, when he saw the poor soul in the ditch** *(Dusts him with feather duster.)*, **his heart went out to him . . .** *(Use paper heart.)* **He bathed his wounds . . .** *(Use cola from backpack.)* **and gave him something to eat . . .** *(Marshmallows)* **Then, he helped the man to his feet and supported him as, together, they walked to the nearest motel.** *(They exit.)* **When the wounded man was made comfortable, his benefactor paid the motel bill in advance, promising that if any more were due, he would pay it on his way back home.**

Only one of the travelers was a true neighbor, despite who and what he seemed to be. *(Starts to leave.)* **I think I'll "go and do thou likewise."** *(Exits, pulling a bag of marshmallows from his pocket.)*

Skit #4

Who Are the Meek?*

INSTRUCTIONS: Five clowns. Clown 3 carries a long, slim balloon. Four clowns enter and sit in four chairs, ready for their Sunday school lesson. Fifth clown, wearing sign that says TEACHER, enters with Bible and takes his place at head of class.

CLOWN 5: **Well, kiddies, today we are going to learn about the Beatitudes.**

CLOWN 1: **We? Are you learning, too?**

CLOWN 2: **We thought you were the teacher.**

CLOWN 5: **I *am* the teacher. See?** *(Models his sign, and clowns are reassured.)* **Now, then, listen while I teach:** *(Reads from Bible.)* **"Blessed are the poor in spirit, for theirs is the kingdom of heaven."** *(Clowns react by pantomiming "poor in spirit," still seated. When they have finished and have agreed that this is a good thought, teacher continues.)*

"Blessed are those who mourn, for they shall be comforted." *(Clowns pantomime "mourn" and "comforted" with huge gestures and wailing. Again, they finish, agreeing that this is a good thought, and teacher continues.)* **"Blessed are the meek, for they shall inherit the earth."** *(Clowns look at one another, but are lost — they cannot interpret "meek.")*

CLOWN 2: **Hey, there! Wait just a little ol' minute, Teach. What's this "meek" stuff? I don't get it.**

CLOWN 3: **Me, neither.**

CLOWN 1: *(Raises hand and waves it.)* **I know! Can I show 'em, Teach? Huh? Can I?** *(TEACHER nods and CLOWN 1 rises; begins pantomiming extreme "shyness" in clown style. Other clowns laugh and make fun.)*

CLOWN 5: **I'm afraid that is not meek.**

CLOWN 4: *(Rises.)* **I got it. *This* is meek.** *(He pantomimes "quiet" by tiptoeing and saying "Shhh." Clowns laugh.)*

*Performance rights for this skit are granted with the purchase of this book. No further permission is needed to adapt or integrate this skit within any performance situation for clown ministry. Excerpted from *Scripture Skits for a Troupe of Clowns* by Janet Litherland. Available from Contemporary Drama Service. See RESOURCES.

CLOWN 2: You gotta be kidding! Someone like that inheriting the earth? No way.

CLOWN 3: Well, then, how about this? *(Asks CLOWN 2 to lie down on the floor and proceeds to hit him with his balloon.)* **You are meek!** *(CLOWN 2 rises and chases CLOWN 3 around room, while CLOWNS 1 and 4 have a private discussion.)*

CLOWN 5: Order! Order, please! *(Clowns obey.)*

CLOWN 4: Hey, Teacher, we got it figured out. Can we show you what *meek* is?

CLOWN 5: *(Nods reluctantly.)* **This is the last demonstration, however. If you still don't have it right, I will teach you. I *am* the teacher, after all.** *(CLOWNS 1 and 4 rise. CLOWN 1 parades proudly around stage; CLOWN 4 follows timidly behind.)*

CLOWN 2: What's that supposed to mean?

CLOWN 3: Looks dumb.

CLOWN 1: *(Points to partner.)* **He's meek. Can't you see it?** *(Clowns laugh.)*

CLOWN 3: He's stupid. I can see that. *(CLOWNS 1, 2, 3 and 4 get into mock battle.)*

CLOWN 5: Stop it! Stop it right now and take your seats. *(Clowns obey.)* **None of your demonstrations, however interesting, have been correct. *Meek* does not mean shy, or quiet, or put upon, or being a mindless follower.**

CLOWN 4: *(With satisfaction)* **It means *pantywaist!*** *(Clowns giggle.)*

CLOWN 5: Certainly not! Meekness is . . . *(Clowns give rapt attention.)* **an awareness of one's own limitations and, thus, a dependence upon God.**

CLOWN 2: Huh?

CLOWN 5: In other words, you realize what you can't do, and you know you need God's presence.

CLOWN 3: Ahh! Then maybe I'm meek after all — I've been praying that God will teach me to do magic *(Or whatever CLOWN 3's specialty is)*. **I'm tired of twisting balloons.**

CLOWN 5: God helps those who help themselves. Have you been practicing?

CLOWN 3: Sure. Want to see? *(Clowns groan.)*

CLOWN 5: Uh, sorry, but time is up. We'll learn more about

this and other Beatitudes next week. *(Clowns and TEACHER scatter, leaving CLOWN 3 thinking he is alone on stage. CLOWN 2, however, has hung back and hovers in background, watching.)*

CLOWN 3: *(Looks upward.)* **Our Father, who art in heaven — I know I'm not much of a magician, but with your help, I'd like to learn. If you find I'm unteachable . . . well, I guess I'll be content twisting balloons. Amen. Let's try it, Lord!** *(He begins a magic trick, timidly at first, then expertly.)*

CLOWN 2: *(To audience)* **Now *that's* meek!** *(He starts applause for his friend and they exit together.)*

Skit #5

The Calling of Disciples*

INSTRUCTIONS: Thirteen clowns and Voice of Jesus (unseen). Clowns are seated in tiny groups on floor, each involved in some sort of activity — fishing, reading, sketching, etc. Voice of Jesus is heard over public address system, causing clowns to quake.

VOICE: In the beginning was the Word, and the Word was with God, and the Word was God.

CLOWNS: *(Looking around)* **"What was that?" "Dunno." "Sure was spooky." "Maybe we imagined it." Etc.** *(They settle down.)*

VOICE: I am the way, the truth and the life: no man cometh unto the Father, but by me.

CLOWNS: *(Jump up. Same kind of discussion. Finally, one clown says, "I'll bet it's God." Others react in a variety of ways — "Yes," "No," "Someone playing a joke," etc. They settle down once more.)*

VOICE: You there — you with the fishing pole.

CLOWN 1: *(Rises, trembling. Looks around.)* **Who, me?**

VOICE: Yes, you. Do you know who I am?

*Performance rights for this skit are granted with the purchase of this book. No further permission is needed to adapt or integrate this skit within any performance situation for clown ministry. Written by Janet Litherland.

CLOWN 1: I . . . uh . . . God, maybe?

VOICE: *(Chuckles.)* **Yes. I am Jesus. Come, be my disciple.**

CLOWN 1: Who, me?

VOICE: You already asked that.

CLOWN 1: But I'm just a . . . a sort of fisherman.

VOICE: I will make you a fisher of men. Is that your brother beside you?

CLOWN 2: *(Rises.)* **Yes, Sir. I'm his brother.**

VOICE: What's your name?

CLOWN 2: *(Gives his own name, such as "Jimbo, the Clown.")*

VOICE: You come, too. And you, there — you two with yo-yos.

CLOWN 3: *(Rises.)* **Who, me?**

CLOWN 4: *(Rises.)* **Who, me?**

VOICE: Is that all you people can say? Yes, you. Will you come and follow me, be my disciples?

CLOWN 3: Who, me?

CLOWN 4: Who, me?

VOICE: *(To CLOWNS 5, 6, 7 and 8)* **What about the four of you there in the corner? Would you be my followers, too, teaching, preaching, or uh, "clowning" in my name? And don't say, "Who, me?"!**

CLOWN 5: But I'm just a juggler. *(Rises.)*

CLOWN 6: And I'm a magician. *(Rises.)*

CLOWN 7: I'm a singer.

CLOWN 6: *(Teases.)* **Sort of.**

CLOWN 8: And I'm only a balloon-twister.

VOICE: *(Sighs.)* **Ah, well . . . it takes all kinds.**

CLOWN 9: *(Rises.)* **Please, Sir, may I be your disciple?**

CLOWN 10: Me, too?

CLOWN 11: And me?

CLOWN 12: *(Rises.)* **I'd be honored, Sir.**

VOICE: Well?

CLOWNS 1-12: Well, what?

VOICE: What about your friend there, *(Indicating CLOWN 13)* **the sad one?**

CLOWN 12: Ah, he's not really sad. He just looks that way. He's really pretty funny.

VOICE: Hey, there, Mr. Sad and Funny. *(CLOWN 13 gestures* *and mouths the words, "Who, me?".)* **I'm glad you didn't say that out loud. Well, what about it?**

CLOWN 13: *(Counts the others.)* **But . . . you already have twelve.**

VOICE: What is that supposed to mean?

CLOWN 13: Everyone knows there are just twelve disciples.

VOICE: Originally, yes. But twelve are hardly enough in these times. I could use twelve thousand times twelve, and even more. It takes many disciples to spread the Gospel.

CLOWNS: *(Jump and clap with delight.)* **"We're going to be disciples!" etc.**

CLOWN 10: *(Steps out of the group.)* **Sir? I mean, Father? Or, uh . . . Lord?**

VOICE: Yes?

CLOWN 10: What do we do now?

VOICE: You get to work. *(Clowns cheer and exit, CLOWN 1 forgetting his fishing pole. Quickly, he returns to retrieve it.)*

CLOWN 1: *(To audience.)* **Whoops! Forgot my fishing pole.** *(Pauses.)* **Wonder if I'll need it to be a fisher of men?** *(Runs Offstage.)*

VOICE: Like I said, it takes all kinds.

Chapter 10:

MORE PERFORMANCE SKITS FOR CLOWN MINISTRY IN CHURCH

Performance scripts for use within a worship service

Top left: Kristin Sideris; right-hand column: all photos of Tim Kehl and family during performance

A growing number of performance skits for clown ministry are being published for use within a worship service. They may be used as sermon supplements or to replace the sermon itself. All of the following nine clown sketches were written by Janet Litherland. Skits #5 - #9 were excerpted from two clown ministry sketch collections entitled *The Clown As Minister I* and *II* available from Contemporary Drama Service of Colorado Springs, CO. (See RESOURCES)

Skit #5

The Clown Healer —

Cast Thy Burden Upon the Lord*

CAST: one clown and one girl

PROPS: **paper, scissors and rope hidden in CLOWN'S pockets**
hat with daisy in it for CLOWN
bag containing four sheets of paper with one word clearly printed on each — LOVE, FAILURE, DEATH, DIVORCE — for GIRL

(GIRL is seated on end of park bench, weeping. Happy CLOWN enters from opposite side, but stops near empty end of bench when he sees GIRL. He is concerned. He tries, very gently and without moving toward her, to get her attention. When she sees him, she turns away, still weeping. He moves a little closer and gets her attention again. He pantomimes, "May I sit with you?" She shows fear and he backs off. He kneels at far end of bench and takes paper from his pocket. He hands it to her. She takes it.)

GIRL: **What's this?** *(Looks it over.)* **An old, crumpled piece of paper . . . What good is it?**

CLOWN: *(Takes paper and carefully folds it, then takes scissors from his pocket and cuts holes in folded paper, producing a lovely snowflake. GIRL smiles, but immediately resumes weeping. CLOWN tries again. He holds out piece of rope.)*

GIRL: *(Shakes head.)* **I don't want it. Can't you see I've got**

*Performance rights for this skit are granted with the purchase of this book. No further permission is needed to adapt or integrate this skit within any performance situation for clown ministry.

problems? A rope won't solve them.

CLOWN: *(Disagrees. He stands, quickly tying rope around his waist, then struts back and forth, showing a "new fashion." GIRL laughs, but quickly catches herself.)*

GIRL: Oh, go away. *(She again weeps.)*

CLOWN: *(Makes a last effort. He kneels and offers his hat.)*

GIRL: *(Kindly)* **It's too big for me. Besides . . . it's ugly.** *(CLOWN shakes his head, still offering hat.)* **What am I to do with it?**

CLOWN: *(Pantomimes weeping and puts his tears into the hat.)*

GIRL: Is that supposed to be funny? *(CLOWN shakes head* no *violently.)* **Well, it's not! Nothing's funny.** *(She reaches into her bag and pulls out the papers one by one, LOVE first.)* **You see this? My boyfriend doesn't love me anymore. He's found someone else.** *(Lays LOVE on bench.)*

And this? *(FAILURE)* **I didn't get the after-school job I applied for. Someone was better qualified. But I needed it! Really needed it!** *(Lays FAILURE on bench.)*

See this? *(DEATH)* **My grandmother . . . d-died last week.** *(Puts DEATH on bench and pulls out DIVORCE.)* **And my parents told me this morning that they're getting a divorce.**

(She crumples DIVORCE and shoves it into the hat CLOWN is still holding.) **Put that in your hat! And this!** *(Crumples LOVE into hat, and bursts into new tears.)*

CLOWN: *(Drops his face into his hat and begins weeping. After a few moments, GIRL looks at him in bewilderment. Slowly, she slides to end of bench near him. Very slowly, she places her hand on his shoulder. He slowly lifts his sad face to her.)*

GIRL: Why . . . why are you crying?

CLOWN: *(Reaches into the hat and sifts the crumpled papers through his fingers.)*

GIRL: My problems? You're crying for my problems? *(Slowly, CLOWN nods.)* **You care?**

CLOWN: *(He nods again. He removes the daisy from his hat and hands it to her. Cautiously, she takes it and slowly puts it in her hair. A smile breaks through her tears. She stands and helps CLOWN to his feet.)*

GIRL: Would you walk with me and be my friend?

CLOWN: *(He nods with a smile, tucking the hatful of problems firmly under his arm. GIRL picks up her bag and they leave together.)*

Skit #6

The Clown Mediator — A Tenebrae Service*

NOTE: Scripture is read by the minister or by a robed narrator. A choir would be helpful for the hymn-singing. Printed programs are an excellent aid to worship.

PROPS: A candelabra holding seven lighted candles is placed Up Center in chancel area. Each clown should develop his own method of extinguishing his candle — between fingers, with hat, by blowing, etc. A crown of thorns is hidden in the costume of one clown.

MUSIC: Suggested hymns can be found in most church hymnals. Similar hymns may be substituted.

CAST: Seven clowns. They play themselves and pantomime the roles of the various biblical characters indicated.

THE SERVICE:

PRELUDE

THE SILENT PROCESSIONAL: *(Clowns enter down Center aisle and take places, three on each side of candelabra, one Down Center.)*

HYMN: "Are Ye Able" *(Center clown, who takes part of JESUS, raises audience and directs singing, himself silent, then seats audience. During this hymn, clowns express confidence in being "able" to be crucified with Christ.)*

*Performance rights for this skit are granted with the purchase of this book. No further permission is needed to adapt or integrate this skit within any performance situation for clown ministry.

THE BETRAYAL: Matthew 26:20-25 *(As minister reads, clowns pantomime the scripture. JUDAS, one clown, then extinguishes the first candle. He feels remorse. He sits down on the floor and remains there until "The Accusation.")*

HYMN: "Alas! and Did My Savior Bleed" *(Clown again leads audience but does not ask its members to rise. NOTE: During each hymn, clowns assume an emotional attitude and stand or sit, as indicated, immobile.)*

THE DESERTION: Matthew 26:30-35 *(Six clowns pantomime the scripture. PETER extinguishes second candle. He, too, feels remorse, sits on floor, and remains seated.)*

HYMN: "Ah, Holy Jesus" *(Clown leads seated audience.)*

THE UNSHARED VIGIL: Luke 22:39-46 *(Five clowns pantomime the scripture. One clown extinguishes third candle, feels remorse, and sits on floor, remaining there.)*

HYMN: "There Is a Green Hill Far Away" *(Clown leads audience.)*

THE ACCUSATION: Mark 14:43-46, 57-65 *(Four remaining clowns and JUDAS pantomime. HIGH PRIEST extinguishes the candle on opposite end. He feels no remorse and does not sit. JUDAS sits on floor.)*

HYMN: "O Sacred Head, Now Wounded" *(Another clown takes over the leading of hymns.)*

THE CRUCIFIXION: Matthew 27:27-36 *(Four clowns pantomime, using the crown of thorns. One of the three remaining clowns extinguishes fifth candle, then turns to lead the hymn. JESUS is on an imaginary cross, and the other clowns are all seated, turned toward him. At this point, they are not feeling as "able" as they did in the beginning.)*

HYMN: "When I Survey the Wondrous Cross"

THE DEATH: Luke 23:44-46 *(Clowns remain seated. JESUS extinguishes the center candle. One clown rises and leads the audience in next hymn. All clowns rise.)*

HYMN: "Were You There"

THE TOMB: John 19:38-42 *(All clowns face away from JESUS, except JOSEPH and NICODEMUS, who enact the drama. JOSEPH extinguishes the remaining candle. All lighting is dimmed until sanctuary is in total darkness.)*

THE HOPE: *(JESUS relights the center candle and removes* *it from the candelabra. One by one, the clowns realize that he has risen from the dead. Each removes a candle and happily lights it from JESUS' candle. Sanctuary lights up slowly as JESUS' light shines among all the people.)*

HYMN: "Fairest Lord Jesus" *(Audience rises and sings.)*

THE SILENT RECESSIONAL: *(Clowns, renewed, exit up Center aisle, carrying their lighted candles. They wave to members of audience as they pass.)*

THE POSTLUDE

Skit #7

The Clown Entertainer:

The Cycle of Life — Three Short Parables*

CAST: four clowns

PROPS: an easel, Centerstage, holding up a large flip-chart; an empty watering can beside the easel

CLOWN 1, the INTERPRETER, stands beside easel and lifts chart cover to expose first page, upon which is printed: *THE SOWER,* followed by the parable *(Mark 4:3-8)*, **paraphrased from a modern interpretive Bible, printed so that the audience can easily read it. CLOWN 2 enters and slowly scatters imaginary grain across the stage** *(with a shuffle-step and pantomimed whistling)*. **He then moves Upstage and turns his back to audience, "freezing" for five seconds to denote passing of time. When he turns to inspect his handiwork, he is surprised, and reacts appropriately to each point made by the parable, beginning with the plot where the birds have taken away the seed.** *(Example: Shakes fists at*

*Performance rights for this skit are granted with the purchase of this book. No further permission is needed to adapt or integrate this skit within any performance situation for clown ministry.

birds. Threatens to shoot.) **He finishes, overjoyed that some seed did fall on good ground and produce abundantly. He praises God in clown fashion** *(dancing, clapping, blowing kisses, etc.)* **and exits joyfully.**

INTERPRETER turns chart to second page: *THE MUSTARD SEED* *(Mark 4:31-32)*. **CLOWN 3 enters and curls into a tiny ball (SEED) on the floor. INTERPRETER picks up watering can and "waters" him** *(SEED reacts)*, **then calls the sun to shine upon him. He steps aside as SEED begins to grow, very slowly, into a large TREE with branches. INTERPRETER approaches the TREE, picks imaginary fruit and eats, then notices hot sun. He sits beneath the TREE and fans himself. TREE helps INTERPRETER to his feet and they shake hands. CLOWN 3 exits.**

INTERPRETER turns to third page: *THE GRAIN OF WHEAT* *(John 12:24)*. **CLOWN 4 enters with three balls to juggle** *(or similar entertainment)*, **but he is distracted by an imaginary patch of dandelions that have gone to seed. He discards the balls and picks the dandelions. He scatters their seeds one by one, by blowing them and waving them, and watches with pleasure as they slowly fall to the ground. Finished, he returns to the balls and performs for the audience** *(no matter how badly)*. **After elaborate bows, he prepares to leave, but is shocked to see pretty new flowers** *(imaginary)* **growing where the seeds had fallen. He hurries to pick them** *(in pantomime)*, **collecting two bouquets, one of which he presents to INTERPRETER. CLOWN 4 exits.**

After placing the imaginary bouquet carefully on the floor, INTERPRETER addresses the audience in pantomime: "We are all like seeds. We are sown *(CLOWN 2 enters)*, **we grow** *(CLOWN 3 enters)*, **we die, and we live again** *(CLOWN 4 enters)*." **INTERPRETER reacts to each entry with a pat on the back or handshake, etc. The clown then encourages the audience to praise God!**

Skit #8

Nothing to Wear*

CAST: one silent clown; one girl; extras (not in clown garb) dressed for Sunday morning

PROPS: oversized watch, oversized comb and feather duster for silent clown

SETTING: Stair steps, Center, to represent front steps to a house. GIRL in jeans and shirt is sitting on steps when curtain opens. *(GIRL watches extras, who pass by two or three at a time, from Left to Right, on their way to church. Some extras have Bibles and may converse about their church and the service ahead, either improvisationally or in pantomime, as they cross the stage. GIRL wistfully takes it all in. Last one to cross is SILENT CLOWN, who enters Left, whistling "Onward Christian Soldiers." GIRL is wide-eyed at the sight of him. He waves to her as he passes, and she giggles aloud, stopping him in his tracks just Right of her. She tries to be serious.)*

GIRL: Where . . . where are you going?

CLOWN: *(Indicates direction and church.)*

GIRL: *(Knows she couldn't have understood correctly.)* **Where?**

CLOWN: *(Is more specific. Pantomimes a steeple, prayer.)*

GIRL: Church? You've gotta be kidding! Clowns don't go to church.

CLOWN: *(Vigorously defends his position.* Everyone *goes to church.)*

GIRL: *(Sighs, thinks of herself.)* **You're wrong. Everyone doesn't go to church.**

CLOWN: *(Shyly asks, in pantomime, "Don't you go to church?")*

GIRL: No. No, I don't.

CLOWN: *(Pantomimes, "Would you like to go with me?")*

GIRL: No! . . . No, I, uh . . . I can't.

CLOWN: *(Pantomimes, "Won't your parents let you?")*

GIRL: My parents? Oh, my parents wouldn't care. But I

*Performance rights for this skit are granted with the purchase of this book. No further permission is needed to adapt or integrate this skit within any performance situation for clown ministry.

can't, anyway.

CLOWN: *(Pantomimes, "Ah, come on. We sing, read the Bible, pray.")*

GIRL: **Yeah. I figured that's what goes on. I hear folks talk. Sounds kind of nice.**

CLOWN: *(Pantomimes shyly, "May I sit down?")*

GIRL: *(Reluctantly)* **Well . . . yeah. Sure, I guess so.** *(She moves over and CLOWN sits beside her.)* **Aren't you afraid you'll be late for church?**

CLOWN: *(Shakes head and points to oversized watch. GIRL giggles.)*

GIRL: **You're funny. I can't believe you're going to church in that get-up.**

CLOWN: *(Elaborately looks at himself — arms, stomach, shoes — then pantomimes, "What's wrong with the way I look?" GIRL turns her head away, shaking it in disbelief, trying to suppress another giggle. CLOWN taps her shoulder. She looks at him. He repeats the question.)*

GIRL: *(Smiles and speaks kindly.)* **Nothing. Nothing is wrong with the way you look. In fact, you look kind of . . . wonderful.**

CLOWN: *(He beams and primps, taking advantage of the compliment.)*

GIRL: **For a clown.** *(CLOWN slumps in defeat. She consoles him.)* **Ah, don't feel bad. What I meant was . . . well, you have to dress up real fancy for church. That's . . . that's why I can't go.** *(She looks away.)*

CLOWN: *(Sits up slowly, aware now of her plight. He rises, crosses Left of her, kneels and pantomimes, "You don't have to dress up fancy. You can go the way you are.")*

GIRL: *(Sighs.)* **You don't know anything, do you? Haven't you seen the folks who pass by here on Sunday mornings? I tell you, they're dressed up. I don't have any dress-up clothes . . . not any.**

CLOWN: *(Helps her to her feet and looks her over. Pantomimes that she looks fine. She smiles and shakes her head, convinced he's a bit crazy. CLOWN gets an idea. He pulls feather duster from pocket and dusts her off, turning her as he dusts. She enjoys his fun. Then he takes oversized comb from other pocket and combs her hair. She laughs. He crosses Right of her and offers his arm, indicating, "We are going to church.")*

GIRL: Me? Go to church with you? *(CLOWN nods.)* **What a pair we'd make!** *(CLOWN nods vigorously, misunderstanding her meaning. She speaks more seriously.)* **Listen, are you sure — really sure — that I could go to church like . . . like this?**

CLOWN: *(Nods firmly. CLOWN then asks in pantomime, "Would you like to?")*

GIRL: Would I like to?! Every Sunday, I sit here wishing I could be part of that crowd. *(CLOWN again offers his arm.)* **You're really serious, aren't you?** *(CLOWN nods.)* **They'll let us in?** *(CLOWN nods again.)* **They won't kick us out because we're . . . different?** *(He shakes his head.)* **You know something? You're the first one who's ever asked me to go to church. And . . . and all of a sudden, I have this funny feeling that if you're with me . . . I can do anything. Wait!** *(She runs up steps.)* **Wait just a minute!** *(She calls Up Center.)* **Mom! I'll see you later — I'm going to church! Yes, that's what I said. I'm going to church! . . . It's all right — I have a new friend who will be with me.**

CLOWN: *(Resumes whistling "Onward Christian Soldiers" as GIRL runs back down the steps, takes his arm, and exits Right with him.)*

Skit #9

The Pastoral Prayer*

CAST: one speaking clown, who takes part of PASTOR — he may wear an open, sleeveless, clown-style robe over his regular clown suit; 10 (or less) silent clowns, who form the CONGREGATION; one unseen reader

*Performance rights for this skit are granted with the purchase of this book. No further permission is needed to adapt or integrate this skit within any performance situation for clown ministry.

PROPS: hidden microphone; background music

SETTING: pulpit, Upstage Left, facing diagonally toward Downstage Right. Chairs are arranged in diagonal rows to face pulpit.

NOTE: Take time with this skit. Don't be afraid of slow, silent pauses.

(Soft, worshipful music plays in the background as congregation enters Right, one or two at a time, pantomiming friendly conversation. When all are in place, PASTOR enters, Upstage Left, and steps behind pulpit.)

PASTOR: Let us pray. *(Everyone bows. As PASTOR prays, he pauses, and one clown — a different clown at each pause — turns in his seat to face audience, though he doesn't look at congregants. He is deep in thought. His thoughts are then heard over hidden microphone. He remains in this position until prayer ends. NOTE: If there are not enough clowns in the group, some may double on lines. They will speak their second lines with a slight change in position.)*

PASTOR: Our heavenly Father, we come to you this morning with thankful hearts, thankful for the many good things you have done for us this week . . . *(FIRST CLOWN turns.)*

READER: Good things? What good things? It's been a lousy week. How can I be thankful for a lousy week?

PASTOR: For the rain that nourishes our crops, we give you thanks . . . *(SECOND CLOWN turns.)*

READER: Yeah. I couldn't get a suntan.

PASTOR: For the homes in which we live and the food we eat, we give you thanks . . . *(THIRD CLOWN turns.)*

READER: Frankly, I can't wait until I'm old enough to move away from home. My folks bug me. Who likes vegetables, anyway?

PASTOR: And now we ask forgiveness for our many sins: the sin of ungratefulness . . . *(FIRST, SECOND and THIRD CLOWNS shift uncomfortably in their seats.)*

READER: Hmmmm. Have I been? Well, maybe. Just a little.

PASTOR: The sin of idolatry . . . *(FOURTH CLOWN turns.)*

READER: No doubt about it. He means Andrew Wallace. Mr. Wallace's hardware store is his idol. He thinks more

of that store than of anything.

PASTOR: The sin of blasphemy . . . *(FIFTH CLOWN turns.)*

READER: Uh, oh. He must have heard about Henry Gobel's blow-up at last night's game. Henry sure let that "ump" have an earful!

PASTOR: The sin of dishonoring the sabbath . . . *(SIXTH CLOWN turns.)*

READER: He must be thinking of Joe Simmons. Joe's playing golf instead of being in church where he ought to be.

PASTOR: The sin of dishonoring our families . . . *(SEVENTH CLOWN turns.)*

READER: Sara Evans has a pair of the sassiest children I've ever seen. If I were Sara, I'd straighten them out in a hurry. Wonder why she doesn't do it?

PASTOR: The sin of adultery . . . *(EIGHTH CLOWN turns.)*

READER: I knew it! I knew sooner or later he'd get after Bob and Carol Smith. It's about time, and I hope they're listening!

PASTOR: The sin of gossip . . . *(NINTH CLOWN turns.)*

READER: Did you hear that, all you Garden Club members? That's all that goes on at meetings any more. Why, last time, there was so much talk that I didn't even get a chance to tell about what happened to — *(PASTOR'S next line cuts off sentence.)*

PASTOR: The sin of coveting . . . *(TENTH CLOWN turns.)*

READER: Coveting? Who covets? I certainly don't covet my neighbor's new swimming pool. I don't even want one. Not one like that, anyway.

PASTOR: And now, heavenly Father, prepare our hearts to receive this morning's text, Matthew 7:3: "Why are we so quick to see fault in our fellow man, yet so slow to see it in ourselves?" . . . *(Clowns, suddenly uncomfortable, begin turning back around, toward pulpit, heads bowed.)* **Show us, Father, the error of our ways, and help us become better people. We pray in the name of Jesus. Amen.** *(All remain with bowed heads, frozen, until curtain closes.)*

Skit #10

Count Your Blessings*

CAST: two clowns

(CLOWN 1 is seated on overturned bucket, Downstage Left. He looks sad and dejected. His left arm is in a sling. CLOWN 2 happily enters Right, carrying a bouquet of balloon flowers. See Chapter 11, "Balloon Art.")

CLOWN 2: *(Notices the downcast state of CLOWN 1.)* **Hey! What's the matter with you? You look lower than a whale's belly.**

CLOWN 1: *(Sighs.)* **Everything's wrong. Nothing's right.**

CLOWN 2: Come on! You're a *clown*. Clowns are supposed to be funny. You can't coax anybody into so much as a giggle when you act like that.

CLOWN 1: *(Stands.)* **Act like that? Act like that! Let me tell you why I'm "acting like that!" My arm is broken. I can't juggle or do magic tricks. I've been laid off from the circus. I can't sing like you can and I sure can't make those goofy flowers!** *(Points to bouquet.)*

To top it all off — it's raining outside, which means no parade, the only thing I *can* do; and I don't have a present for my mother. Today's her birthday.

CLOWN 2: Gee, that's too bad. Mothers are kind of touchy about birthdays. *(CLOWN 1 sighs loudly.)* **OK. You've got a lot of problems, but you're the one who's always preaching about looking on the bright side. Why, you were singing a hymn just the other day about counting your blessings.**

CLOWN 1: Yeah. "Name Them One by One."

CLOWN 2: Why don't you try taking a little of your own advice? Count your blessings.

CLOWN 1: *(Points to broken arm.)* **I don't have anything to count with. These fingers don't work. Remember?**

CLOWN 2: *(Sighs in exasperation.)* **All right. Let's use these flowers.** *(Holds out one flower.)* **Name a blessing.**

CLOWN 1: Well . . . I have a nice family. *(CLOWN 2 puts flower*

*Performance rights for this skit are granted with the purchase of this book. No further permission is needed to adapt or integrate this skit within any performance situation for clown ministry.

into CLOWN 1's right hand.) **And . . . I have terrific friends.** *(CLOWN 2 gives him another flower.)* **And . . . except for this dumb arm, I'm healthy.** *(Receives another flower.)* **Hmmm . . .**

CLOWN 2: Come on, you can do better than that.

CLOWN 1: Oh, yeah . . . I have a brand new clown suit! *(Models. CLOWN 2 shakes his head, but gives CLOWN 1 a flower anyway.)*

CLOWN 2: What else?

CLOWN 1: OK . . . I had an answer to prayer about my sister. *(Another flower.)* **And . . . my best friend is sharing meals with me, since I'm out of work and can't cook.**

CLOWN 2: I'd say that's a double blessing. *(Hands him two flowers.)* **Anything else?**

CLOWN 1: *(Thinks.)* **. . . Oh, yeah. I've got a job in a parade next Saturday, if it doesn't rain. Pray it doesn't rain!**

CLOWN 2: *(Gives him the last flower.)* **See there? You have a lot of blessings. I had eight flowers, so that means you have eight blessings.**

CLOWN 1: Make that nine.

CLOWN 2: You've thought of another one?

CLOWN 1: Yeah. *(Holds up bouquet.)* **Now I have a present for my mother's birthday!** *(Runs off Left.)*

CLOWN 2: Hey! *(Chases after him.)*

Skit #11

What is Peace?*

CAST: three clowns and a narrator

PROPS: three easels, each holding a piece of white posterboard
two large stick-on hearts (may be made from construction paper and backed with two-way tape)
one gold medal (a large gold stick-on circle)

SETTING: Easels are Centerstage and Centerstage Left, facing audience. A clown is stationed at each easel. Tray of crayons is on a small table downstage of easels. NARRATOR (playing an

*Performance rights for this skit are granted with the purchase of this book. No further permission is needed to adapt or integrate this skit within any performance situation for clown ministry.

elderly lady) stands Downstage Right, wearing a large badge that says *JUDGE*. NARRATOR has gold medal. Stick-on hearts are in pockets of CLOWN 3.

NARRATOR: *(Reads from script.)* **Welcome, ladies and gentlemen, to the first annual "Peace Poster Contest," sponsored by our local Arts Guild, of which I am the . . . ahem . . . president. Three outstanding artists have been invited to participate.** *(Indicates clowns. They primp and nod to audience.)* **They will attempt, before your very eyes, to illustrate the meaning of *peace*, as I present several profound thoughts on the subject.**

Our first contestant is ________________ *(CLOWN 1's name)*.

CLOWN 1: *(Bows with a flourish as NARRATOR encourages applause. He checks his posterboard, picks through the crayons, then stands beside his easel.)*

NARRATOR: This artist has been creating beautiful work for more than fifteen years!

Our next contestant has come all the way from ________________ *(Name of nearest large city)*. **He is the winner of numerous awards and is, of course, looking for the gold medal** *(Holds it up)* **just like everyone else. Let's welcome ________________** *(CLOWN 2's name)*. *(Encourages applause.)*

CLOWN 2: *(Looks over the crayons.)*

NARRATOR: Our third contestant is a newcomer to this area. Frankly, I haven't seen any of his work, but he comes highly recommended. I'm told that his latest creation graces the Red Bathroom at the White House! Give a hearty welcome to ________________ *(CLOWN 3's name)*. *(Applause)*

And now, ladies and gentlemen, the moment you've all been waiting for. Artists, assume your positions. *(Clowns each select a crayon and stand at respective easels.)* **On your mark . . . get set . . .** *(Giggles)* **create!** *(Clowns begin working. See diagrams on page 82.)*

CLOWN 3: *(Merely scribbles, putting large, colorful blobs on his posterboard. Note: A large* red *blob must appear on the bottom center portion.)*

NARRATOR: *(Giggles.)* **Ooh! Isn't this exciting?! While our artists are busy, busy, busy, let me tell you a little about peace. Our guild thought this would be a perfect subject for the contest, since we are all at peace, one with another.** *(CLOWNS 1 and 2 reach for the same crayon and begin bickering, in pantomime, over it.)* **Well . . . most of us.** *(CLOWN 1 finally breaks crayon, so that they may share.)*

ALL CLOWNS: *(During NARRATOR'S speech, clowns continue to create. When appropriate, they react to elements of the speech. CLOWNS 1 and 2 sneak peeks at others' work, but CLOWN 3 is oblivious to the activity around him. He steps back, measures with thumb, and gives the impression that he is working very hard on his blobs.)*

NARRATOR: *(Continues.)* **We are speaking, of course, of *peace*, as in *peace of God* . . . not *piece of pie*.** *(Giggles.)*

CLOWN 2: *(Gives her a slow stare.)*

NARRATOR: **Now for the profound.** *(NARRATOR emotes slowly and deliberately.)* **Peace is the absence of conflict. It is a state of tranquility and quiet joy. When I think of peace, I think of a beautiful sunset** *(CLOWN 1 reacts, because that is what he is drawing)* **with warm, glowing colors.**

I also think of a quiet lake *(CLOWN 2 reacts — he is drawing a lake)* **with soft blues and greens. Peace is a gentle breeze, a serene heart.**

CLOWNS 1 & 2: *(Begin to shake their heads at CLOWN 3. His loud blobs have nothing to do with* peace *as they see it.)*

NARRATOR: **I now quote from the scriptures: "To the counselors of peace is joy." Proverbs 12:20. "For ye shall go out with joy, and be led forth with peace." Isaiah 55:12. "The mountains shall bring peace to the people." Psalm 72:3. "And on earth peace, good will toward men." Luke 2:14. "Let us therefore follow after the things which make for peace." Romans 14:19.**

ALL CLOWNS: *(During scripture reading, clowns finish their artwork and stand by their posters, anxiously awaiting announcement of the winner. NARRATOR finishes with a flourish that definitely says, "the end," but nobody applauds. Clowns catch on and encourage audience to applaud the NARRATOR.)*

NARRATOR: *(Basks in the glory.)* **Thank you, thank you,**

thank you! . . . Now for the moment we've all been waiting for. Which of our talented artists will win the Gold Medal of Peace? *(Crosses to easels and examines each poster. She oohs and aahs over #1 and #2, but stops short at #3.)*

Uh . . . excuse me, Mr. . . . uh . . . *(Consults her notes, then calls CLOWN 3 by name.)* **Am I missing something here? This sort of looks like . . . uh . . . a jot and a tittle.** *(Giggles nervously.)*

CLOWN 3: *(Shakes head vigorously, points to poster, then to self.)*

NARRATOR: Ah . . . A self-portrait?

CLOWN 3: *(Nods earnestly. Other clowns nod knowingly and make signs that CLOWN 3 is crazy.)*

NARRATOR: But it looks all . . . kind of . . . nervous.

CLOWN 3: *(Shakes his head, moving hands to "prayer" position over his chest. He then takes black crayon and adds lines — see Figure 4 on page 82.)*

NARRATOR: Oh . . . But I still don't understand.

CLOWN 3: *(Adds heart — see Figure 5 on page 82 — and pantomimes, "My heart has peace." NARRATOR looks puzzled. CLOWN 3 adds* JESUS *to heart — Figure 6 on page 82.)*

NARRATOR: *(Finally understands.)* **Ohhh! You have the peace of Jesus in your heart.** *(CLOWN 3 nods happily.)* **Well, now . . . It seems that you have chosen to portray the *ultimate* peace — the peace of God. For that, you win . . .** *(Holds up medal.)* **Yes . . . the Gold Medal!** *(Sticks it on CLOWN 3's easel and encourages applause.)*

ALL CLOWNS: *(CLOWNS 1 and 2 are too dejected to applaud. CLOWN 3 notices, takes two hearts from his pocket and sticks them on the easels of the other clowns. Their spirits are lifted and all shake hands.)*

NARRATOR: Ah, yes. This is truly an illustration *(Indicates CLOWN 3's poster)* **and a demonstration** *(Indicates clowns)* **of *peace*. Mission accomplished!** *(NARRATOR encourages audience to applaud.)*

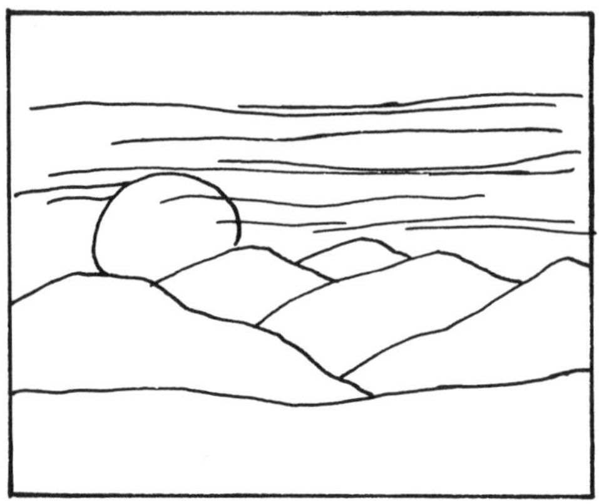

Fig. 1 **CLOWN #1**

Fig. 2 **CLOWN #2**

Fig. 3 **CLOWN #3**

Fig. 4 **CLOWN #3 adds face**

Fig. 5 **CLOWN #3 adds heart**

Fig. 6 **CLOWN #3 adds JESUS**

Skit #12

Food for Thought*

CAST: three clowns

(CLOWNS 1 and 2 enter, cross to chairs, Downstage Center, and sit. Each takes a paperback book out of his pocket and begins to eat it. CLOWN 3 enters and stands Right of other clowns.)

CLOWN 3: Our scripture lesson for today is entitled, "Food for Thought," or perhaps more appropriately, *(Gestures to the book-eaters)* **"Thought for Food." Hear these words from Ezekiel:**

CLOWN 1: "And when I looked, behold, a hand was sent to me, and a book was in it. Then I did eat it; and it was in my mouth as honey for sweetness." *(Licks lips, pats tummy and enjoys his book.)*

CLOWN 3: Hear these words from Revelation:

CLOWN 2: "And I took the little book out of the angel's hand, and ate it up; and as soon as I had eaten it, my belly was bitter. *(Pantomimes illness and indigestion.)*

CLOWN 3: And now, hear these words from the Song of Solomon: "I went down into the garden of *nuts* *(Indicates the other clowns)* **to see the fruits of the valley!"** *(Quickly exits Right.)*

CLOWNS 1 & 2: Hey! You set us up! *(They run after CLOWN 3.)* **That wasn't fair! You *clown!***

Skit #13

Joke Time*

CAST: two clowns

(CLOWN 1 enters. He wears baseball cap. Is tossing a baseball and catching it in his fielder's glove.)

CLOWN 2: *(Joins him onstage.)* **Hey! Did you know that the Bible talks about baseball?**

*Performance rights for these skits are granted with the purchase of this book. No further permission is needed to adapt or integrate these skits within any performance situation for clown ministry.

CLOWN 1: Oh yeah? Where?

CLOWN 2: Genesis 1:1: "In the big inning . . . "

CLOWN 1: *(Reaction. Pause.)* **I've got one for you. What Bible character played tennis?**

CLOWN 2: Tennis? . . . I don't know. Who was it?

CLOWN 1: Joseph. He served in Pharaoh's courts.

CLOWN 2: *(Reaction. Pause.)* **I can top that. Who was the teensy tiniest man in the Bible?**

CLOWN 1: Gimme a hint.

CLOWN 2: He was a disciple.

CLOWN 1: A disciple! Oh, no.

CLOWN 2: Oh, *yes*. It was Peter. He slept on his watch.

CLOWN 1: *(Reaction. Pause.)* **OK. Here's one you'll miss for sure. How many *anteaters* did Moses take in the ark?**

CLOWN 2: That's easy. He took two of everything.

CLOWN 1: Wrong! Moses didn't take any. It was *Noah!* *(They exit, laughing and back-slapping.)*

Chapter 11:

BALLOON ART

How to entertain an audience by making a wide variety of objects from balloons

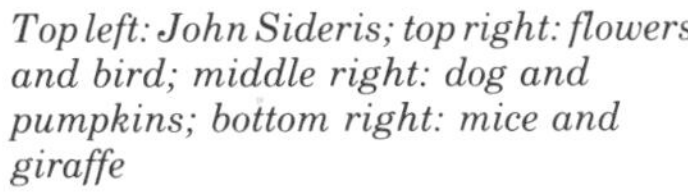

Top left: John Sideris; top right: flowers and bird; middle right: dog and pumpkins; bottom right: mice and giraffe

Any clown technique or skill requires time, patience and practice. Some require more than others. One of the easiest to learn, yet most effective, is "balloon art" or "balloon-twisting." Balloons are lightweight and easily concealed in the wardrobe. They are colorful eye-catchers and can be used as clown gifts after the audience has had the fun of watching the balloon designs take shape.

What equipment is needed? A balloon and some air! Many clowns use a small pump for the difficult-to-inflate balloons, but tiny giggles and hearty laughs can also grow out of the clown's struggle to inflate balloons with his own hot air. Either way, there is a trick to inflating: stretch the balloon several times before beginning. If the balloon is long and narrow, pinch it about five inches from the valve end and stretch gently while blowing. When inflation begins, release the pinch, letting air into the remainder of the balloon.

For twisting, balloons must be strong and flexible. For this reason, it is best to order balloons especially made for this purpose. (Resource centers are listed at the end of this chapter.) There are three basic types: the apple balloon, which takes its name from the fruit it becomes; the bee balloon, which has an end resembling a stinger; and the pencil balloon, which is long and pencil-thin. Apple and bee balloons are always two-colored, one color on the nipple end and another on the valve (blowing) end. Pencil balloons come in a variety of solid colors.

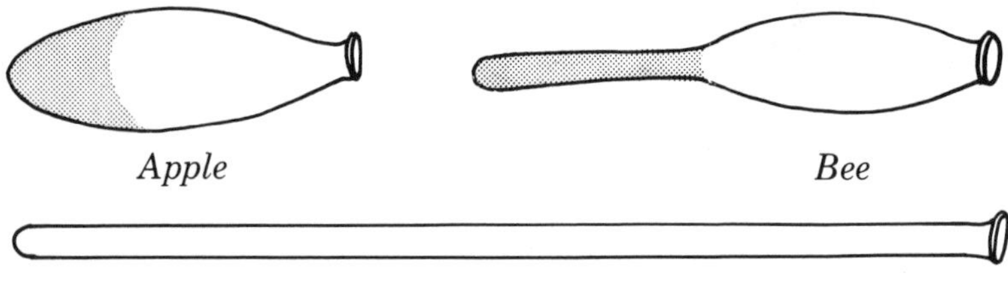

Following are five basic designs and two variations. Remember, dear clown, technique takes time, patience and, most of all, *practice*. Happy ballooning!

APPLE

1. Inflate an apple balloon to 4" and tie the valve end.

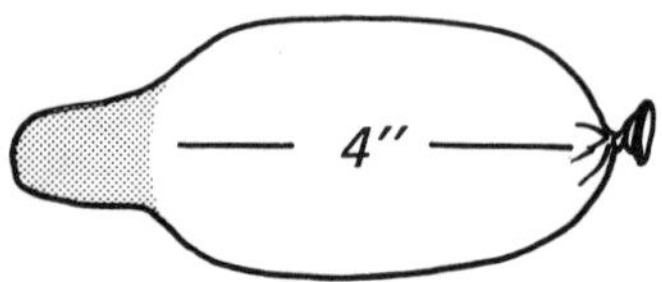

2. Holding nipple between fingers of left hand, wet the index finger of right hand and push valve into nipple. (A wet finger is easier to retrieve.) Pinch nipple and valve together, removing finger of right hand.

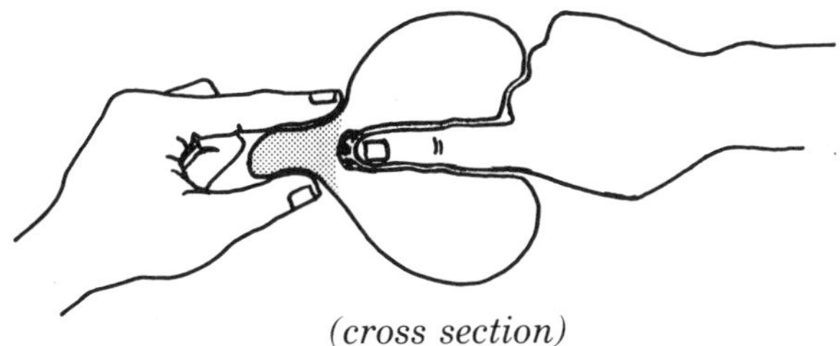

(cross section)

3. Take balloon in right hand and pull base away from nipple and valve, still pinched together in left hand. Twist base five times. Release.

(cross section) *Apple*

Variation: PUMPKIN

Follow same steps as for **Apple**, using a bee balloon.

Pumpkin

BASIC SKULL OR BUBBLE

1. Inflate a bee balloon to 5" and tie the valve end.

2. Squeeze in center, forcing some of the air toward nipple. Twist five times. (This is called a "bubble" twist.)

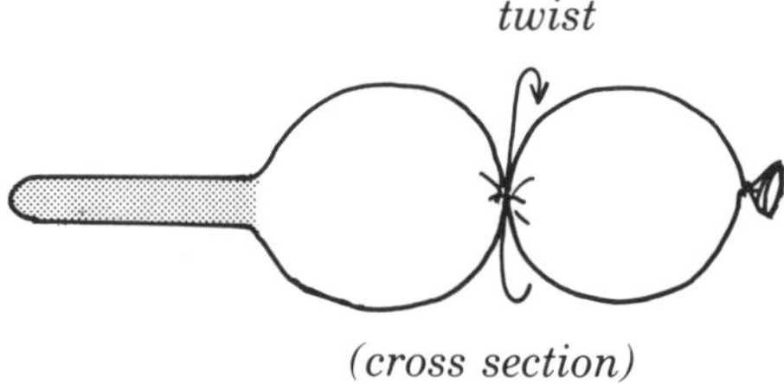

(cross section)

3. Tie valve and nipple together.

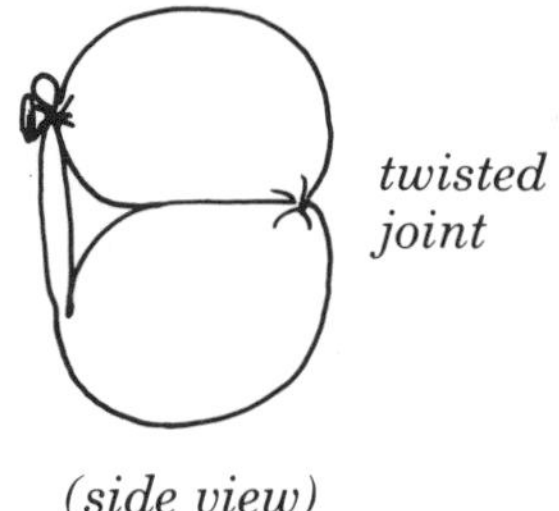

(side view)

4. This is the basic shape. It is now ready for decoration — message, painted face, taped-on wings, ears, etc. — wherever the imagination leads. Colored markers work best for drawing. Be sure they are non-toxic if the balloon is to be a clown gift.

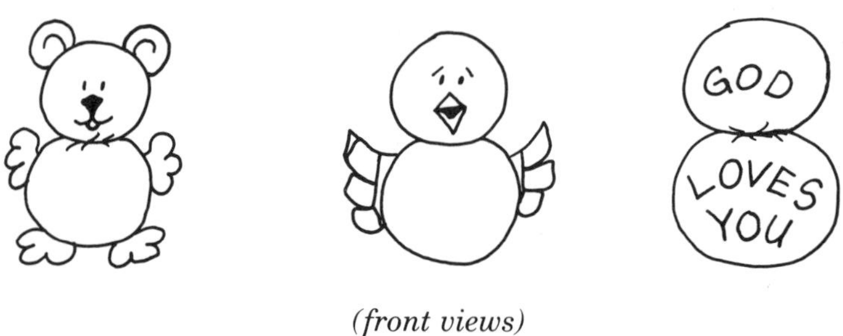

(front views)

FLOWER

1. Inflate a pencil balloon to 3" and tie the valve end. (Pencil balloons are extremely difficult to inflate. Have patience!)

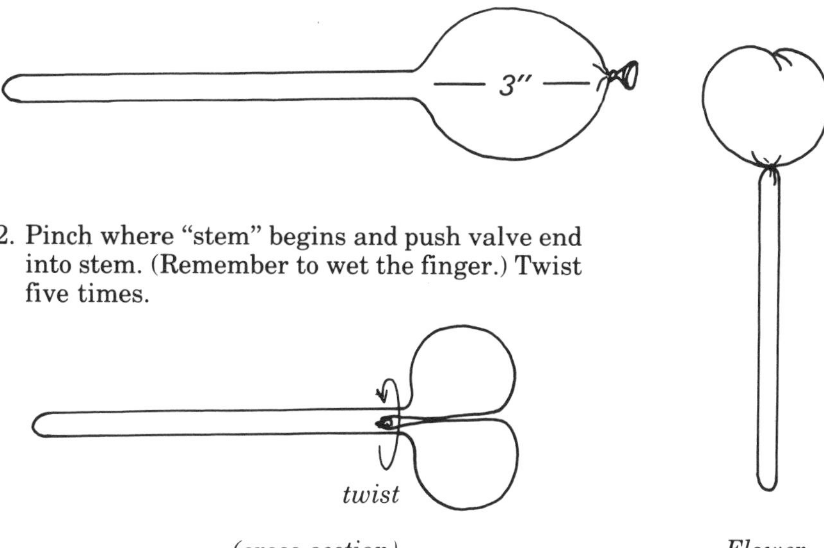

2. Pinch where "stem" begins and push valve end into stem. (Remember to wet the finger.) Twist five times.

(cross section) *Flower*

Uses: Many flowers make a colorful bouquet. One or more may decorate a clown's hat. By folding the stem and squeezing it between the fingers, the flower becomes a "wilting" flower. Use this trick when someone tries to sniff it or blow on it.

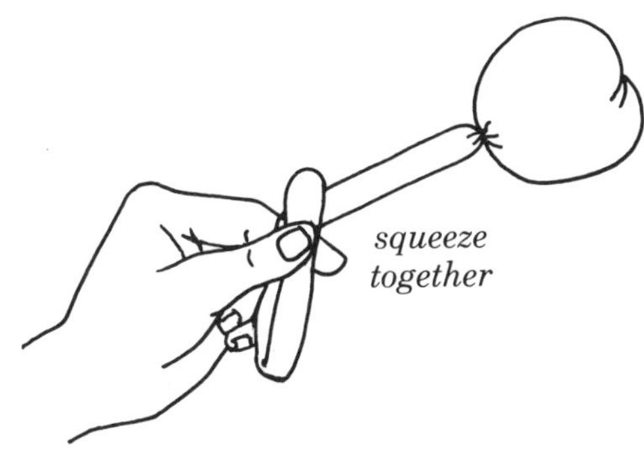

MOUSE

1. Inflate a pencil balloon to 7" and tie the valve end.

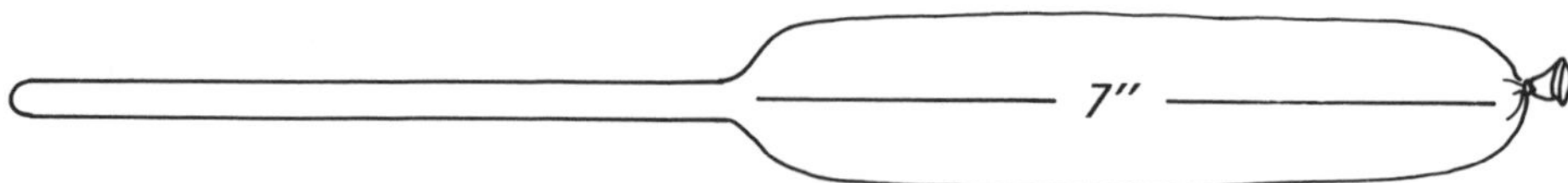

2. Bubble twist (four times) into four identically sized bubbles at valve end.

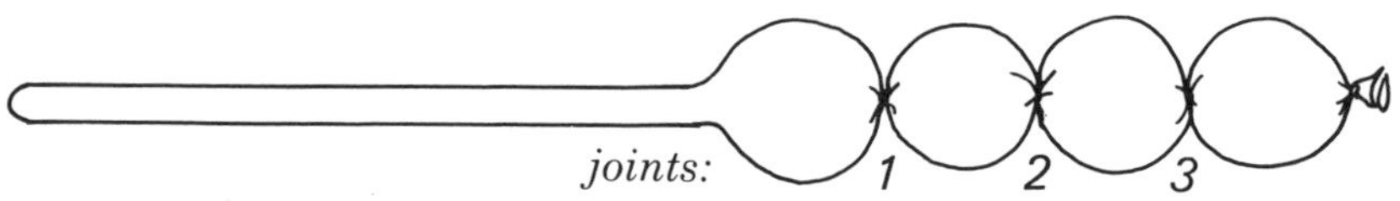

3. Fold, matching joint 1 to joint 3.

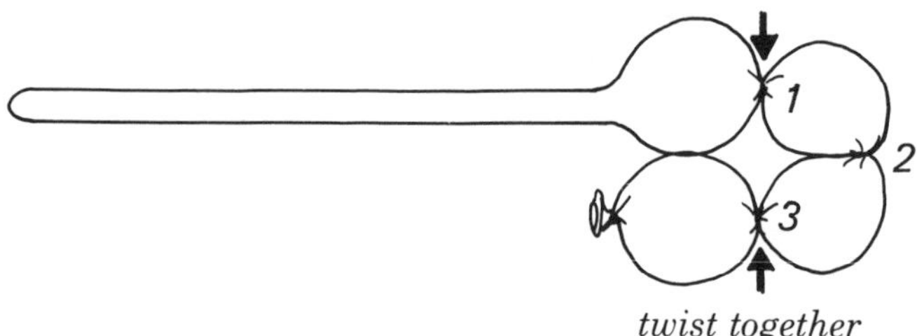

4. Twist joints 1 and 3 together (see above).

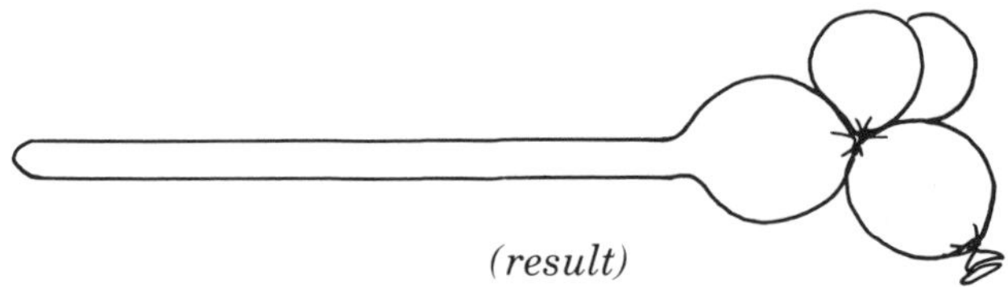

(result)

5. Bend tail downward to shape, and mouse will sit on clown's finger.

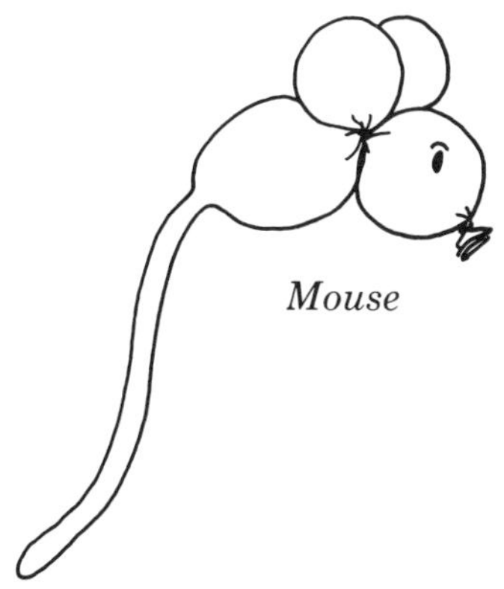

Mouse

DOG

1. Inflate pencil balloon to within 5" of end and tie.

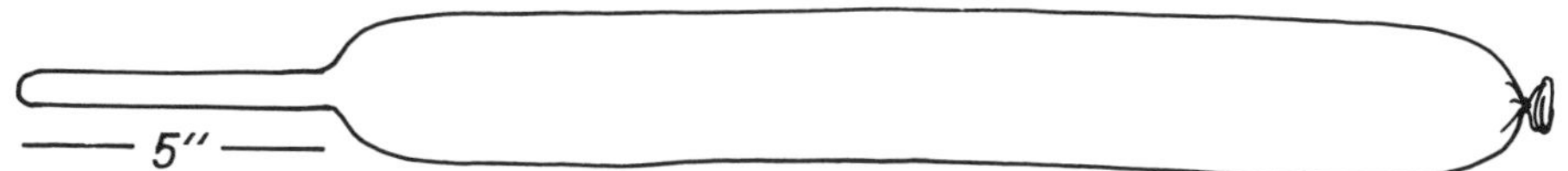

2. Follow steps 2 and 3 under **Mouse**.

3. Twist three more bubbles, slightly larger.

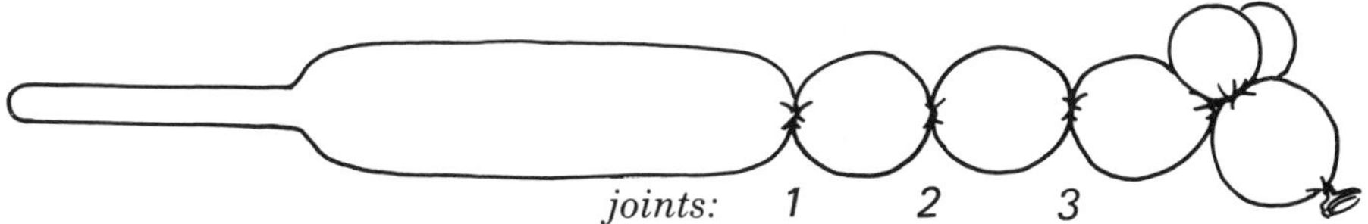

4. Fold joint 3 to joint 1 and twist.

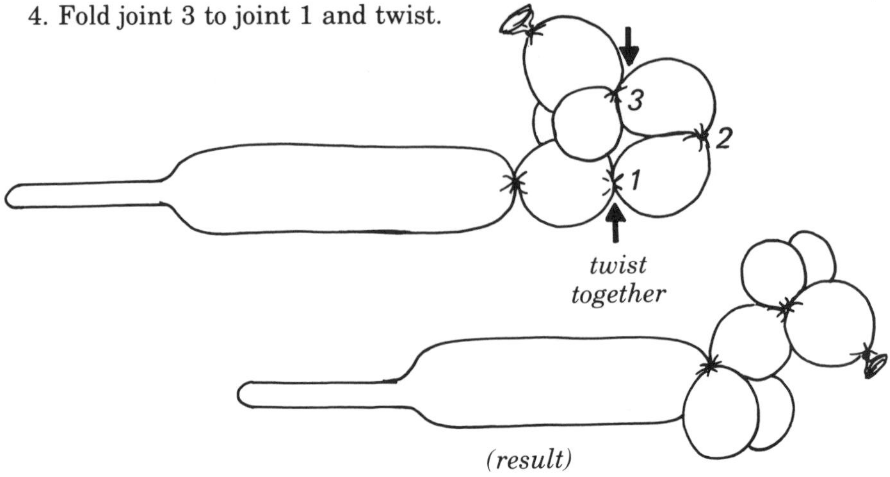

5. Leaving a long bubble for body, twist three more bubbles near nipple end. (Nipple becomes smaller as bubbles force air into it.)

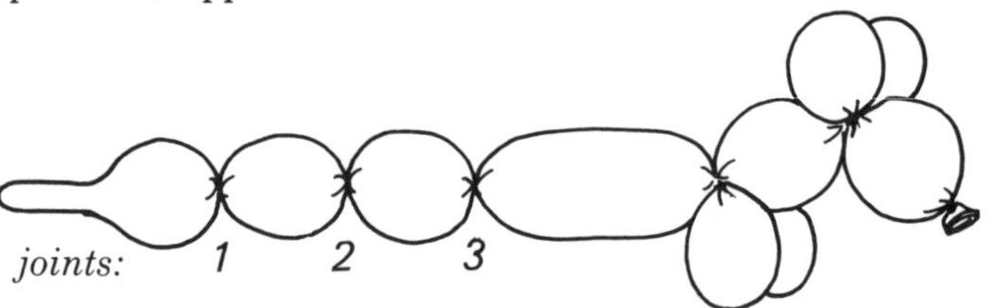

6. Fold joint 1 to joint 3 and twist.

Variation: GIRAFFE

Construct as **Dog**, except make long neck, instead of long body. Draw spots.

Giraffe

Mark Clayton ("Markie") is a young clown minister who specializes in balloon art. He very kindly served as resource person for this chapter. His story is included in Chapter 12: "Caring and Sharing Clowns."

RESOURCES

Balloon pumps and balloons for balloon art may be purchased from the following companies and from many novelty and theater specialty shops:

Show-Biz Services
1735 E. 26th Street
Brooklyn, NY 11229

Recreation Novelty
221-23 Park Avenue
Baltimore, MD 21201

The Circus Clowns
3556 Nicollet Avenue
Minneapolis, MN 55408

"Love" balloons are also available. These balloons come in different shapes and sizes and have *love* printed on them. They are for sharing.

Chapter 12:

CARING AND SHARING CLOWNS

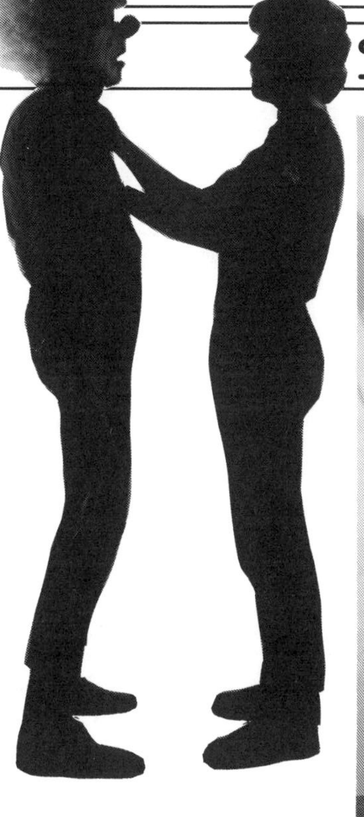

Clown ministers tell how they came to be clowns for Christ

Top left: Charlie Lewis and Jeff Simms; top right: Philip Noble (Rainbow); lower right: Marcia Graham (Popcorn) and the Right Reverend O'Kelly Whitaker (photo by Cathy Gibbons, Syracuse, New York)

Several active clown ministers from various parts of the United States — and even one from Scotland — very generously agreed to share a little of themselves — thoughts, ideas and experiences. These personal testimonies are offered to struggling clown ministers everywhere, with the hope and prayer that they may receive inspiration and encouragement.

FLOYD SHAFFER

Socataco

How it began . . . There were no flashes of lightning, no claps of thunder. In fact, my conception of a clown ministry happened so gently and so slowly that I hardly knew what was happening.

One key moment occurred when I discovered the unique relationship of the word *clod,* from which the word *clown* was derived. The nearest equivalent term in the New Testament was the Greek word *doulos* — a lowly form of servant, a slave, called upon to do the most menial tasks, which others would not do. The way in which the word *clod* was used and the way in which the word *doulos* was used were strangely close, to the point of being intertwined.

I smiled when I realized that whenever Jesus called upon followers to become like servants, the word *doulos* was always used. What a mind-boggling concept, I thought. Our Lord, in a strange way, was pointing out an affirmation of clowning . . . or rather what clowns could be and were intended to be — lowly and earth-like, childlike and playful, vulnerable and trusting, giving up power in order to raise others to power.

From that beginning, my life was redirected. Early years were spent in developing ideas and skills. In 1970, an entire worship, including Holy Communion, was celebrated without saying a word, using clown black-outs and routines as a communicative form.

Since then, I've been able to reach many different groups — over 40 Christian denominations, psychotherapists, theological schools, colleges, deaf ministries, gerontologists, marriage enrichment weekends, personal growth, humor therapy. I continue to be half-time in a Lutheran congregation, while the other half of my time is spent in my own growing probe of the various applications of the clown in ministry.

ERNIE LIEBIG
Happy, the Clown

My venture in clowning began in 1953, when I became involved in a clown club sponsored by the City Recreation Department in Tyler, Texas, where I lived. The club's major function was to provide clowns for community-sponsored parades and for the annual City-Wide Playground Circus. From this beginning, "Happy, the Clown" was created. It did not take long for me to realize as a Christian that this could become a tool to share our Lord with others. Working in Christian recreation provided an opportunity to form a church-sponsored clown unit at First Baptist Church, Tyler, Texas. Thus began a ministry for Christ through clowning that continues to the present for me.

The clown ministry involvement today is multi-faceted. It has developed from entertainment to proclaiming the Gospel of Christ in worship settings. Happy uses clown magic to provide entertainment, involvement of others and spiritual truths. He is also blessed by having a loving partner, his wife, Jean, who presents the character "J.J., the Puppet." Together, wherever possible, they take the love of Christ to children of all ages through magic, song and stories.

The ministry includes entertainment to children in hospitals, senior adults in retirement homes, vacation Bible schools, mission schools and trips, day camps, youth and adult camps, church banquets, picnics, fun dramas, music ministry and special events. Street ministry is conducted at malls, fairs and parades, with distribution of gospel tracts. The opportunity to promote an activity or an event as a clown provides an endless list. Our clown gospel ministry includes programs for Sunday schools and pulpit ministry in children's and adults' worship.

In addition, Happy conducts clown seminars for the Southern Baptist Convention on local, state and national levels. He has conducted seminars at Southwest Baptist Theological Seminary, Fort Worth, Texas, and several colleges. He is author of numerous articles and papers on clowning and is co-author, with his wife, Jean, of the Christian clowning book, *Clowning Is*.

Clowning has provided another avenue to reach people for Christ. The clown, being a universal symbol, communicates to all, regardless of age, race, color or language. To be a Christian clown means that the love of Christ shines through the make-up and costume, and as you work with people, the love of Christ can be splashed on them.

Many times as I visit children in hospitals, just Happy's presence, allowing them to touch and talk with him, is sufficient medicine to cheer up a downcast spirit. One does not have to quote scripture to sick children for them to know of God's love. They will know it through you, the clown for Christ.

Several memorable events stand out as I thank the Lord for ministry through clowning. One experience took place south of Monterey, Mexico. We were on a mission trip with youth and adults and were to conduct a week's activities of Bible study and recreation at an orphanage. The missionary wanted to invite people from the surrounding villages to attend, but felt the task impossible. Eight of our clown group donned costumes and make-up. We loaded our pockets with candy and printed invitations in Spanish and began a seven-mile trek to put out the good news. Unable to speak their language, we were nonetheless accepted by the villagers, since they recognized the happy countenances of our clowns. As we walked from village to village, many children and adults joined us. We felt like pied pipers. Our crowd, which numbered 38 people when we started, numbered well over 400 when we returned to the orphanage. The missionaries said that never before had such a large group of people gathered in their immediate area. During the week, many children and adults came to know the Lord. God had used a *payaso* (clown) to bring them together. "God hath chosen the foolish things of the world to confound the wise." (I Corinthians 1:27)

The joy of clowning and bringing happiness to others far outweighs the burden of grease paint, perspiration and physical tiredness. Another instance I would like to share is something that remains vivid in my memory. This true story happened while I was standing on a street corner, working the crowd with free balloons and suckers, publicizing the Southern Baptist Convention Church Recreation Department. Out of the crowd, a small beautiful girl approached, holding hands with her parents. Her mother asked her if she would like to see Happy, the Clown. Without hesitation, she replied very much in the affirmative. When she was within arm's reach of the clown, Happy realized this small 5-year-old was totally blind. He knelt down and spoke with her and told her that he was Happy, the Clown. He took her hands in his and "showed" her his oversized nose, his wiry red hair and the make-up on his face. She felt the large shoes and costume. Finishing her touching, she said, with happiness in her voice, "I really see you, Happy!" Her parents smiled and responded with tears in their eyes, "Yes, Happy is beautiful." Happy thought, "How many reach out and touch someone . . . but never see?" The same is true of our Lord Jesus. Some reach but never find. I'm glad our Lord has a place for clowns.

CAROL J. PHIPPS
Servo Servin

In 1971, the lady with whom I lived volunteered me to "clown" (wear a classical clown costume) for the many children expected to attend an annual senior adult bazaar, sponsored by a missionary society. I was more than glad to fool around as I kept these yearning youngsters too busy to get into trouble. In that classical clown garb, I did not wear make-up, but had wire-rim glasses and wore an artificial Christmas tree for a hat. That was fun.

During the next several years, various opportunities were given to me to clown around using the same classical outfit, handmade by the women of that missionary society. At that time, my clowning was mostly leading in games and other fun activities while masquerading in clown garb without make-up. Cleverness and agility were always assets around the bouncing children, and the "gift of gab" helped fill time.

While serving as a church extension summer missionary in Chicago in 1975, I experimented with historical clown characters. Three face types surfaced that summer while I was clowning for backyard Bible clubs, parades, a carnival and gangs of children on the streets of Uptown Chicago. They were the whiteface, the character clown predominately in red, and the character clown predominantly in black. In a short time, I began favoring the character clown. The hobo character fit my inner yearnings to be an example of Christ in my world — the down-and-outer, the cast-out slapped by life. A personal theology of clowning grew up around the clown name I conjured that same year — "Servo Servin," or "I serve, serving."

A few related truths were already set in my mind on automatic rewind. First, Jesus, my example, came to serve and not to be served. Second, God gave us the talents we have, and he expects us to multiply them while serving him (Matthew 25). Third, we are ambassadors for Christ, light and salt, giving hope to the world. The lives of Abraham and Sarah, Joseph, David, Peter and Paul, as depicted in the Bible, have greatly influenced my personal theology and my clowning. Avner Eisenberg, the mime who is billed "The Eccentric," helped me, while he was teaching at the University of Louisville, develop some basic clowning skills.

The real conversion of my clowning to a viable ministry resulted from a friend's challenge. She asked me to "clown my testimony" — how I became a follower of Christ. At first, I was speechless and doubtful. But, brainstorming the humor in my Christian conversion, based on Acts 16, opened a whole new world for me, as well as a new approach to clowning. The sketch developed portraying my conversion has been a very popular one with religious audiences, as it incorporates drama, storytelling, audience participation and local church humor. Since then, my script has largely been the Bible story and stories retold in a dramatic storytelling style, with general clowning around (gags, balloon-sculpting, juggling, simple magic, puppets). My style is also to involve the audience with acting and singing and/or chanting. It continues to be a truly human experience with divine blessings. The National Clown, Mime, Puppet and Dance Ministry Workshops and the National Storytelling Workshops have been valuable to me.

In June, 1982, God invited me to *enjoy ministry,* as I had known it through the clown, Servo, on a full-time scale — to allow him to use all that he had been cultivating and refining in a more total ministry than I had known before. Servo Servin (my *ideal* self) fans love to a warm flame. This love, elicited by Servo, has slowly been graciously and amazingly applied to my entire person. A creeping crescendo of wholeness has been taking over my life as the *clown* envelopes people and life itself. Since I was 12, I had involved myself, according to my ability and God's grace, in local church ministries. In part-time and full-time church staff positions, I served all ages in Christian education. There was joy, limited. There was not fulfillment. "Sell what you have. Get free, come follow me," said Jesus. "Equipping To Serve" (E.T.S.) was born in the midst of a great house and yard sale. Since June, 1982, my partner, Karen Heath, and I have traveled more than 18,000 miles equipping folks to serve and entertaining for the glory of God. We lead workshops, seminars and retreats in the creative arts of clowning, puppetry, balloon sculpting, juggling, biblical storytelling and deaf signing. We have experienced personal healing as we have entertained small children on dialysis machines, international children and parents being oriented to the United States, and crippled children in special hospitals.

A piece of God's workmanship created to do good works, I am perpetually a student, truth-teller, evangelist, listener, consoler and teacher. My hope is to equip everyone I can for God's sake and his kingdom. Though I am a fool and weak, God is glorified while his people are edified through the clown. (Ephesians 4:11-12; I Corinthians 4:10)

Ideas:

- carnival booth for artistic clown: The clown sketches willing patrons. Everyone sketched by the clown becomes a clown on paper.
- activity called "Make the Sound": Before an audience, mime various animals, emotions, falls, etc., to warm up the audience. Ask the audience to make the sound evoked by what they see. Then mime a short skit and have them spontaneously call out the sound they see; i.e., mime a bird — audience makes flapping sounds or bird calls, etc. Mime fear — audience screeches or expresses fear of some kind. Mime tripping and falling — audience responds vocally as they see it.

KAREN HEATH
Fingers

Since my teen years, I wanted to be involved in professional ministry. Toward that goal, I studied in college and seminary; however, I was not attracted to the jobs that were available. For four years, I worked as an administrative secretary in a denominational organization, but it was not a ministry for me. I spent nights and weekends doing volunteer work at church to have contact with people in a personal ministry, and I went back to school for a degree in counseling, but ran out of money and incentive. It was not what I wanted . . . But I could not describe what I wanted.

Somehow, I always had the feeling that the hours spent in volunteer work were more valuable than any others. They included unusual and exciting experiences and, in time, introduced me to clown ministry.

Carol Phipps and I lived and worked together for several years. Eventually, we clowned together. I met Carol at seminary and watched her clowning develop into an art. She added and refined skills consistently, but her clowning was a ministry from the start.

My first clowning experience came in 1979, when Carol and I entertained about 200 women and girls belonging to a church organization. The audience seemed to enjoy the program, but I didn't. I was too nervous. Carol invited me to clown with her many times after that and I tried. The costume and make-up made me look like a “real clown,” but I didn’t feel like one. About a year later, I learned why; I attended a week of workshops on clowning ministry and related arts. I learned from many people that week, but Bill Peckham, Methodist minister and founder of “The Holy Fools” clown ministry, had the greatest impact on my development. Instead of trying to put on a clown, I began to let the clown character evolve within me. In a completely new clown face and costume, I experienced exciting growth as I expressed myself through clowning. The make-up and costume changed as radically as my approach to clowning.

“Fingers” is the name of my clown character, who is a symbol of my desire to minister in a unique way. My ministry has to be centered around people, touching their lives and meeting their special needs. Fingers does that, touching people emotionally and spiritually in simple heartfelt ways, and touching physically those who need a hand on the shoulder, a hug or reassurance that someone loves and cares. Fingers is also a symbol of my desire to minister to the large number of deaf people who depend on hands to communicate with each other and the rest of the world.

Full-time ministry has become a reality for me through Fingers, as a partner in the new venture, “Equipping To Serve.” Feeling strongly the need to share with others what we have learned, Carol Phipps and I are teaching others to use the tools of clowning, mime, puppets, juggling, balloon-sculpting and basic drama. Launching this freelance ministry has been a journey of faith and adventure, travel and service. Without regrets, I have, with Carol, adopted a completely different life style in order to minister in the capacity God has opened for me.

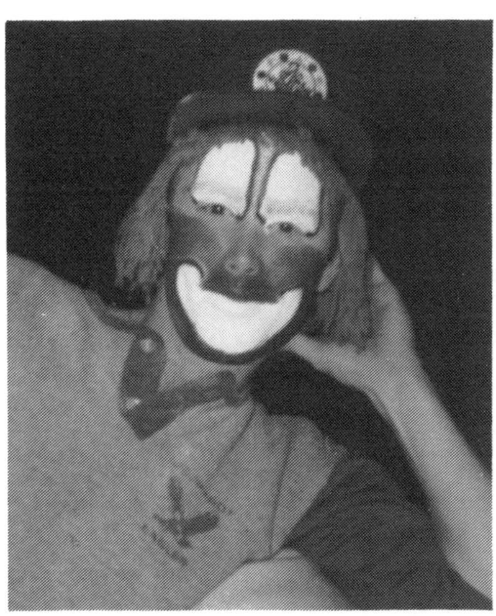

MARK CLAYTON
Markie

Clown ministry is relatively new for me, having only been a clown for a little more than two years. However, the gifts of God that I have experienced while clowning could fill any person’s lifetime. As our world changes daily and seems to modernize by the minute, we, as God’s ministers, must change also, to meet the needs of the people. After having heard and actually seen what a tremendous impact a clown can have on others, I was convinced that clown ministry was a good, efficient way to minister to people. As I applied the clown make-up and personality for the first time, I had a very special feeling. That feeling has stayed with me ever since, growing and growing. It involves love, warmth, concern, empathy, dedication, happiness and joy. To put all of these God-given feelings into one person is just fantastic. To me, there is no greater reward than to see an angry person smile, a stoical person shed a tear, or a person weary of life find new inspiration. All of these things and many more can be accomplished through a clown's smile, actions and emotions.

Why am I a clown? Well, God has shown me that a smile or a simple hand of genuine affection is worth many words. I want to spread the love of God in a way that a person will never forget. No matter if it's several seconds or several hours, as a Christian clown, I feel that I am a true producer of happiness.

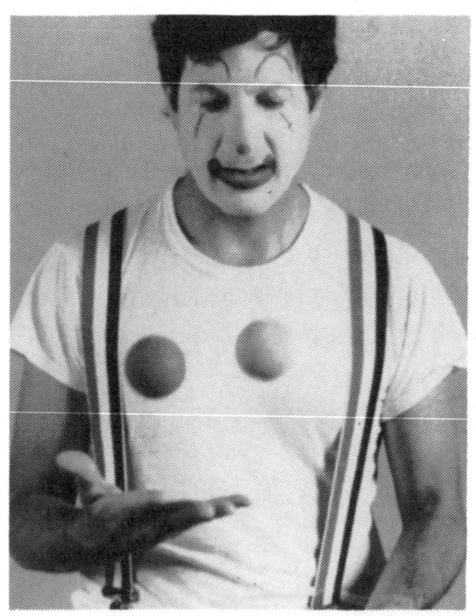

TOM WOODWARD

Uncle Billy's Pocket Circus

The clowning I do best is street clowning — that is, setting up at a festival or street corner and doing "Uncle Billy's Pocket Circus" — or what I do from what used to be a two-person street show. The Pocket Circus now consists of juggling, fire-eating, some magic and several mime pieces. What I am trying to do through this work is to share nonverbally what is, for me, the heart of the Christian vision. I do not feel the need to be explicit about words or symbols which stand behind what I do. I let the experience stand for itself and for whatever others bring to it. In some sense, that's in the tradition of parable-teaching in Christian scripture — the heart of the teaching is religious, but without religious language.

Some of the themes I explore in my street clowning are greed, heroism, sin, redemption, grace and the biblical sense of justice. What I try to do is invite people into the experience of these things and provide a framework, without defining or limiting the experience. That does not work for everyone, but it is the way I have come to do things.

I got into this work through the doing of it. I had spent some time on college campuses, where I had served in whiteface, but that was on registration days when I went one-on-one with the incoming students once a year. But when I was working as Episcopal chaplain at the University of North Carolina, I met a young man who had dropped out of law school in order to devote all his time to his juggling. He was a remarkable person and a fabulous juggler. (We ended Uncle Billy's with his juggling three ping pong balls out of his mouth!) Kenny Kaye and I soon became a team. For him, it was partly due to financial situation; for me, it was an opportunity for joy. We began working the campus in Chapel Hill for dollars, quarters and dimes, and soon branched out to other universities and festivals, parks, gatherings of all sorts. People liked what we did. We counted it all joy (and several dollar bills). One of the sad parts in moving from North Carolina was leaving Kenny. He continues to juggle and perform on his own and with various groups.

A second part of using clowning as a ministry has been clowning for registering students during registration week in the fall. Every fall, I go out on the campus (I have worked as a college chaplain since being ordained 20 years ago), and go one-on-one with as many students as possible, trying to bring joy and acceptance on a day which, on the whole, has not been pleasant for them. I always do this on the day the first-year students register, because they have the hardest time of it — classes closed out, difficult choices, homesickness. I have loved it. Every year, this has been one of the most special days.

It has been only lately that I have become involved in what many see as the mainstay of clown ministry, calling on people in hospitals and nursing homes. A really lovely person in Madison, Wisconsin, Pat Ryan, wanted to do something special with the elderly and handicapped. She proposed to me and to Barbara Quirk, an outreach nurse at one of the hospitals, that we attempt to create a clown troupe consisting primarily of the elderly and the handicapped. What a challenge and what a joy this has been!

What has happened has been the formation of the troupe, "The Care-Fools," a terrific collection of elderly and handicapped people and their friends and supporters who clown all over the city. We have elderly, mentally handicapped, aphasiacs, people with cerebral palsy, others with difficulty walking, talking, getting from one day to the next, and recovering alcoholics. Every time they go out clowning, miracles happen — mostly to the people for whom they clown. Our clowns in wheelchairs can minister in a way I had never before thought possible.

I have heard dozens of stories months (and now years) after the miracles have happened (and have seen some myself). One of my favorites involves Lydell Swenson, who, with his form and severity of cerebral palsy, is unable to speak or gesture. A nurse told me of one of her patients who had just had both legs amputated. He was severely depressed and was being watched carefully as a possible suicide. But one day, she said, into his room was wheeled this strange guy with a funny-looking hat and clown make-up. He looked at our patient and our patient looked back — they were simply together, without saying a word.

What happened, she told me, was miraculous. Our patient said the next day that something snapped. "Here I was in bed feeling sorry for myself and thinking seriously about suicide because my useful life was over, when into my room came this strange clown who couldn't talk and didn't have use of either arms or legs. He was just there — with a fraction of what I have left, going through a hospital trying to cheer people up! And I got to thinking, 'Maybe this isn't the end of my life; maybe it is just the beginning!' "

The best thing about the "Care-Fools" is that clowning has turned them, the recipients of care for so much of their lives, into the *care-givers!*

I think it is really important for people to widen the whole sense of what clown ministry is. I look forward to the days when we have clown troupes in prisons and in corporations. And we need to be aware of all the spiritual gifts as we think about clowning. Isaiah, Jeremiah and Hosea used the medium of clowning and pantomime to speak the difficult words of prophecy to a complacent world. We need at least that from some prophetic clowns in our own times. Go for it.

PHILIP NOBLE
Rainbow

Philip Noble ("Rainbow") has served as a mission priest with the Anglican Church in New Guinea and as rector of two small Episcopal churches in Glasgow, Scotland. He is now attached to the Episcopal Church in Prestwick, Scotland, with freedom to travel as called to spread the "Good News." He travels as Rainbow, a Christian clown who specializes in string art and in *origami,* the Japanese art of paper-folding.

"The clown character that the Lord has freed in me is named Rainbow, as the sign of the new covenant and the disclosing of the wonder of the spectrum of white light," Philip says. "My understanding of the clown is perhaps close to the 'holy fool,' or child. Rainbow is a silent clown. He is very gentle and open to all that is going on. He never pushes forward, is very cautious, yet makes the most wonderful discoveries. He is not clever, though he finds God's world to be full of delight and surprise.

"A crumpled piece of paper seems to fold itself into a bird; a rope becomes an elaborate string pattern with just a little twist. Often, Rainbow himself isn't very good at things, but his friend, Jaffa the Squirrel (a glove puppet), helps him and shows him how. Sometimes Rainbow sets a scene by playing simple tunes on a guitar, kazoo or lyre.

"There is, for me, a real need for the life of the clown to be consistent. That is, if the wig and paint are missing, the person still reacts in the same way to the life situations he meets. One person said to me, 'Oh, it must be easy to be an extrovert when you are hidden under all the make-up.' I've thought a lot about this, and believe it to be the opposite. The make-up doesn't hide the real clown — it shows up what is already there."

Philip's clown ministry group at St. Ninian's Episcopal Church in Prestwick, Scotland, was invited to "add color" for the visit of Prince Charles and Princess Di. They also took part in a large gathering of The Salvation Army. Philip is now into "bubble art" and says that America's Joy® dishwashing liquid (unfortunately not available in the United Kingdom) makes the most wonderful, long-lasting, easy-to-work-with bubbles!

Following are two of Philip's skits or routines. The first was inspired by the people of New Guinea. "Nearly everyone in Papua, New Guinea, knew how to make string figures," says Philip, "though they were cautious about admitting it for fear of being thought 'childish' by Westerners. I was able to travel through many remote areas during my work, and collected over 150 different patterns, several with stories or songs. Some of these designs involved the use of toes or ears, or took two or three people to complete."

The Prodigal Frog*

CLOWNS NEEDED: two

PROCEDURE: First, make the rope frog design, then begin the story. One clown may tell the story while the other remains silent; or both clowns may remain silent while a narrator (live or tape-recorded) reads the story.

MATERIAL NEEDED: a 25-foot length of soft green rope

THE ROPE TRICK:

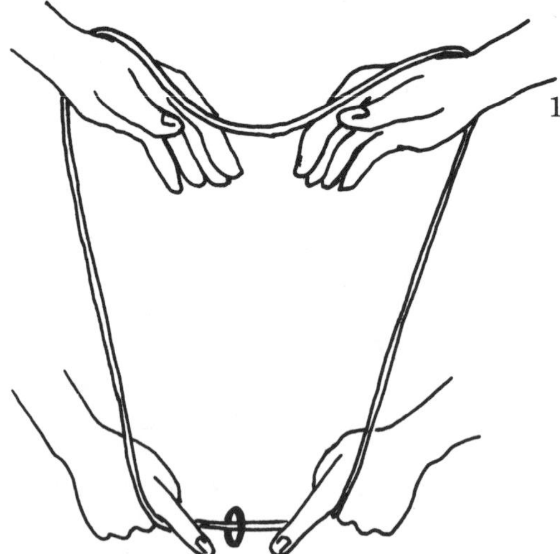

1. Begin with the loop held down by your helper. His index fingers should be about 6 inches apart and ready to let the string slip freely around them. The rest of the loop is placed on your wrists so that a part of the loop hangs down in the middle.

*Performance rights for this skit are granted with the purchase of this book. No further permission is needed to adapt or integrate this skit within any performance situation for clown ministry.

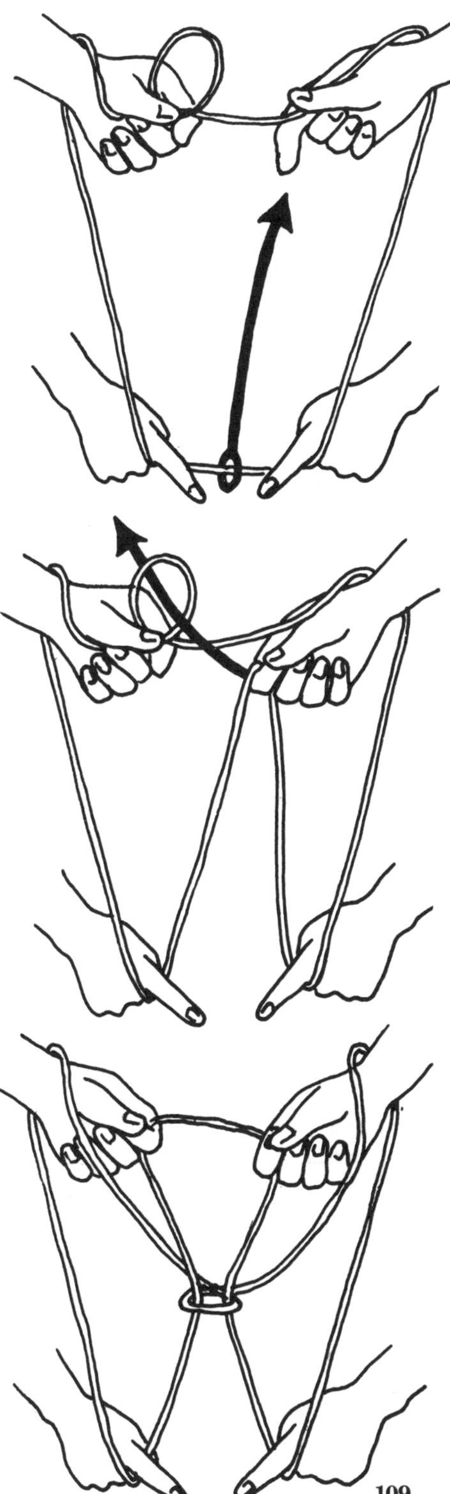

2. With the right hand, hold the string at the point marked in Step 1 and make a small loop with the left hand. Keep the string on the wrists.

3. Now pull *up* the piece of string lying between your helper's index fingers. Keep the string on the wrists. Pass this pulled-up loop of string through the small circle of string held in the left fingers.

4. At the same time, drop the circle of string and take hold of the pushed-through loop with both left and right hands. The loops on the wrists must not be allowed to drop off during these moves.

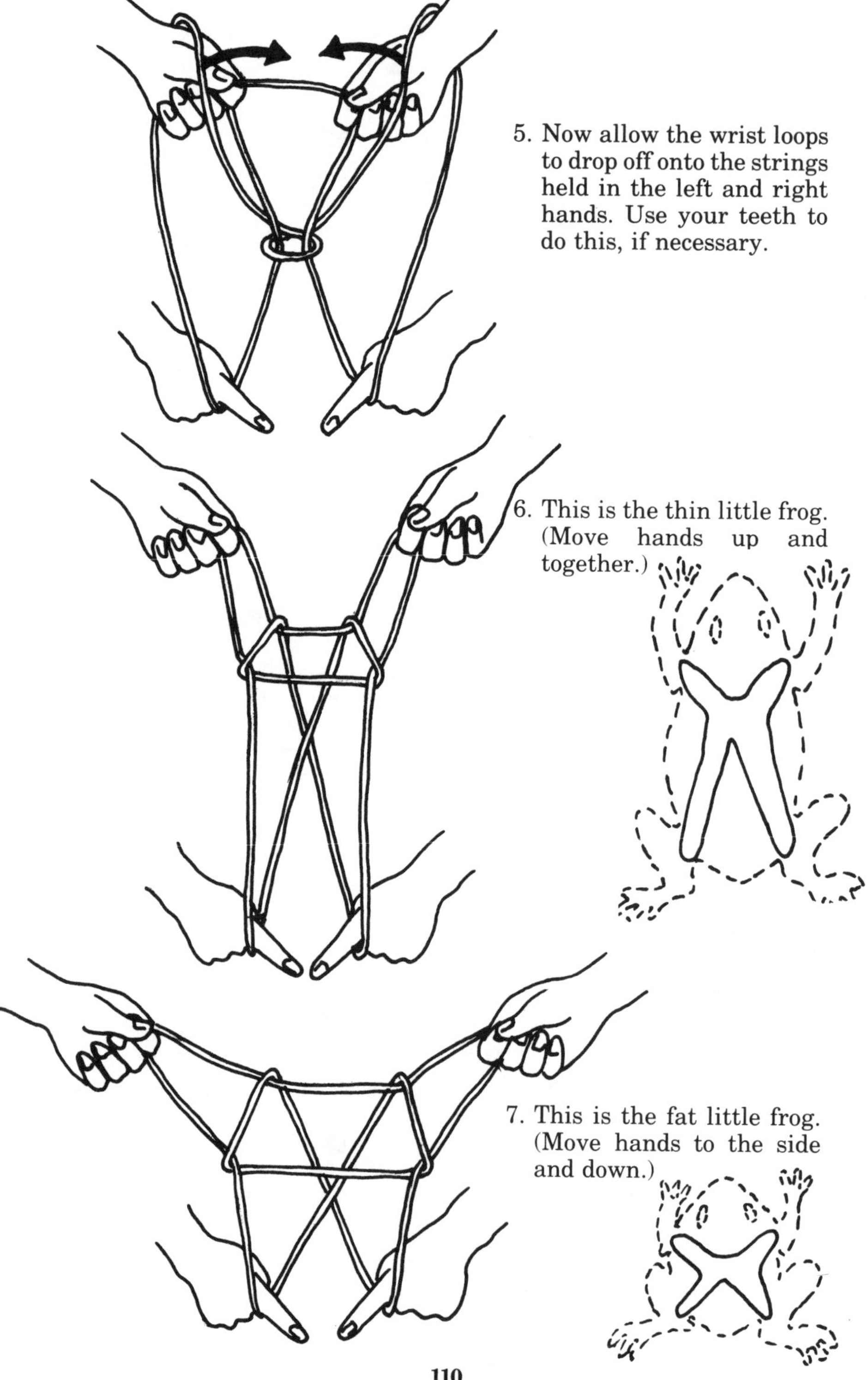

5. Now allow the wrist loops to drop off onto the strings held in the left and right hands. Use your teeth to do this, if necessary.

6. This is the thin little frog. (Move hands up and together.)

7. This is the fat little frog. (Move hands to the side and down.)

THE STORY: In a land a long, long way from here, there once lived a little frog. It was a hot land of palm trees and beautiful beaches called Papua, New Guinea.

One day, the little frog's father said, "Well, little frog, now that you are twelve years old, you can come and help us in the food garden."

But the little frog was lazy and said, "I won't."

So his father said, "If you do not help in the garden, there is no food for you."

That night, the little frog went hungry. The next day, the father again asked the little frog to come and work in the garden. Again, the frog refused. And again, he had no dinner.

As this went on, day by day, the stubborn little frog grew thinner and thinner. *(Move hands together with little tugs on the design. The frog will get thin.)*

Finally, the little frog was so thin he nearly wasted away. But still he wouldn't work. Instead, he had a good idea. "I know," he thought. "I'll go to my grandmother in the next village; she'll give me food to eat." So, next day, the little frog got into his small canoe and paddled down the coast to the nearby village.

When his grandmother saw him, she gave him a big dinner, and he got a bit fatter. *(Move hands apart, allowing the shape to enlarge slightly.)*

Each day, she gave him a good big meal, and each day, he grew fatter and fatter, until he was enormous! He had never been that fat before. *(During this part of the story, slowly draw hands apart, and the center of the design will fatten.)*

Then one day, his grandmother said, "Little frog, now that you're fit and strong, will you help me in the garden? I am an old woman now and do find it hard, working to feed two mouths."

But again, the little frog said, "I won't."

So his grandmother sternly warned him, "No work, no food."

Each day, she asked if he would help, and each day, he again said, "I won't." And he went without his dinner.

The little frog grew thinner and thinner. *(Move hands together and up to make the shape thin.)*

Finally, one day when the little frog was so thin you could see right through him *(Show)*, **he came to his senses and thought, "If I am to work, I would rather be with my own family than in this strange village." So he got back into his little canoe and paddled home.**

His father came running to meet him and cuddled him, refusing to let him speak until he had given him a special, delicious meal.

Then the little frog said, "Father, I've been wrong, and I do want to work. Do you think I can?"

"Of course," said the father. "But not for a few days yet. Just rest."

When the little frog finally did go out to work, he found that he got very hot and tired . . . and a little thinner *(Show)*, **yet every evening, he came home and had a good meal and got a little fatter** *(Show)*.

So, he never got really fat *(Show)* **or really thin** *(Show)* **again.** *(Return hands to medium-size position.)*

The Captive Is Set Free*

CAST: two clowns. CLOWN 1 is gentle and compassionate. On his back hangs a sign, *JESUS LIVES*. Sign should not be visible to audience until end of skit. CLOWN 2 is hardened and hurting. Dresses in dark colors.

PROPS: square piece of paper, loop of string, large handkerchief and grease pencil or felt-tipped marker (CLOWN 1); scissors (CLOWN 2); three bean bags on floor, Left

CLOWN 2: Stands Centerstage Right, facing audience, feet apart, arms crossed over chest, head down.

CLOWN 1: Enters Stage Left, happily whistling and humming. Notices CLOWN 2, realizes he is hurting, and has an idea. Pulls a square piece of paper from his clothing and folds it into a bird. With delight, he pulls the

*Performance rights for this skit are granted with the purchase of this book. No further permission is needed to adapt or integrate this skit within any performance situation for clown ministry.

tail, and the wings flap. *(Directions for folding a bird may be found in many books on paper-folding, including* ***Paper Folding for Beginners****, by William D. Murray and Francis J. Rigney, published by William Gannon. Practice many times until technique is smooth.)*

When bird is complete, CLOWN 1 crosses to CLOWN 2 and taps him on the shoulder to get his attention. He shows the bird, then presents it to CLOWN 2.

CLOWN 2: Half-smiles. He accepts the bird, pulls tail to make the wings flap, but keeps on pulling and tears the bird. He throws it down and returns to his closed position.

CLOWN 1: Slowly and gently gathers the torn paper and places it next to his heart. He then has another idea. Smiling, he takes a string loop from his pocket. Making a cat's cradle, he approaches CLOWN 2. *(Cat's cradle is formed by winding loop once around each palm, then, with Right middle finger, picking up palm string on Left hand. Left middle finger picks up palm string of Right hand.)* **CLOWN 1 invites CLOWN 2 to transfer the cradle to his own hands.**

CLOWN 2: Appears agreeable, but as CLOWN 1 looks toward audience, pleased, CLOWN 2 quickly takes scissors from his pocket and snips through the strings. Goes back to his closed position.

CLOWN 1: Is visibly hurt, but soon has another idea. Pulls out large handkerchief and wraps it around his Right arm. With grease pencil or felt-tipped marker, he puts two dots on the back of his Right hand. He then cradles his Right arm ("baby") in his Left arm. *(See diagrams on next two pages.)* **Makes baby sounds as he approaches CLOWN 2.**

CLOWN 2: Shows a little more interest, but suddenly pulls the handkerchief away and uses it to blow his nose loudly.

CLOWN 1: Gives up. Crosses Left to bean bags, picks them up, and begins to juggle.

CLOWN 2: Slowly peeks at action. But every time CLOWN 1 looks his way, he hides his head.

CLOWN 1: Tosses one bag high and to Right, where CLOWN 2 catches it instinctively.

CLOWN 2: **Stands still, staring at the bag he has caught.**

CLOWN 1: **Crosses Right, encouraging CLOWN 2 to toss the bag up and catch it.**

CLOWN 2: **Tosses and catches. Begins to show genuine interest.**

CLOWN 1: **Puts his arm around shoulder of CLOWN 2. They exit Right, pantomiming the mechanics of juggling. At this time, the sign on CLOWN 1's back, *JESUS LIVES*, becomes visible to audience.**

HANDKERCHIEF BABY:

1. Hold handkerchief at corner between right thumb and index finger. Drape it over the back of the arm.

2. With left hand, wind handkerchief twice around the right arm. Make right hand into a fist and adjust the handkerchief to come over the top of "baby's" head.

3. Add eyes with pen.

DAVID EBEL
Happy-Go-Litely

David Ebel ("Happy-Go-Litely") is a "hug-collector" who has traveled over 115,000 miles collecting hugs from children. He has an extra special reason to hug on the Lord's behalf. David was born with defective legs and attended the University of Detroit on a scholarship for the handicapped. While there, he experienced severe emotional problems that led to a nervous breakdown and dependency on alcohol and drugs. One night in a church service (he had gone to "make fun of it"), the Lord spoke to David and he listened. "God revitalized my life!" he says. Immediately, he was healed of his nervous condition and of his alcohol and drug dependency. His ministry, since that moment, has been an upbeat, enthusiastic thank-you to God.

Since he accepted Christ, David has been involved in outreach ministry (ministry to the deaf, evangelism training, counseling at coffee houses and in jails) in Michigan, Illinois and Wisconsin.

David, his wife Diane, their daughter Ruth, and their sons Joshua and Jessie Daniel have recently formed "Love Family Ministries" — this in addition to David's full-time work as State Evangelist for the Church of God in Georgia where he specializes in children's ministries. David and Diane ("Lazy Daisy") have also opened a professional clown company in Atlanta called "Big Top Quality Clowns." A delightful new character, developed by their children, is "Amazin' Praisin' Raisin" who sings, "I Heard It Through the Prayerline."

David's clown character, Happy-Go-Litely, is a preaching clown with a fast-paced presentation of the Gospel through magic, balloon art and object lessons aimed at leading listeners to a personal relationship with the Lord. Says David, "Happy-Go-Litely tries to love everyone and cause them to laugh and enjoy life and to realize that the joy they feel comes from Jesus."

Happy-Go-Litely means "happy to be going for the Light of the World." The divergent arrows on Happy-Go-Litely's face symbolize two choices: be a fool for the Lord . . . or a fool for yourself.

"God has a sense of humor," says David. "He produced the anteater, the duckbilled platypus and the laughing hyena!" David, in his Gospel magic, produces live things, too. His hat often has a rabbit or a chicken in it. And sometimes (though never when in clown costume), he produces Jezebel, his 4½-foot boa constrictor.

Following are three of the techniques David uses in his "Kids' Krusades."

Offering*

Before the service begins, "bankers" are positioned in one corner of the room to make change, because *pennies only* are used for the offering. After the offertory prayer, a tape recorder plays cheerful, bouncing calliope music, while the children stream *(In an orderly manner)* **to the front of the room. Here, they pour their pennies into brightly painted buckets that hang from the crossbar of a huge scale. One bucket is for boys, one for girls. Children love to see which bucket tips the scale and who "wins." They cheer and clap when the scale tips from one side to the other, and Happy-Go-Litely reminds them again and again that their fun in giving grows out of praise and love for God.**

*Performance rights for this offering idea are granted with the purchase of this book. No further permission is needed to adapt or integrate this idea within any performance situation for clown ministry.

Object Lesson*

PROPS: lamp (no shade), with lamp cord hidden so that children cannot see that it isn't plugged in; 60-watt bulb; extension cord; a working light socket; large Easter basket

(Using props, CLOWN talks to children, encouraging their participation. Included here are the responses children most frequently give to Happy-Go-Litely's questions and comments.)

CLOWN: What does it take to make a car go?

CHILDREN: Gas! Oil! Water!

CLOWN: It also takes electricity. The car uses a battery to get the spark of electricity that it needs to make it go. *(Holds up bulb.)* **What does it take to make this bulb go?**

CHILDREN: Electricity!

CLOWN: Right. Electricity is a kind of power. If I take the bulb and put it into this lamp *(Demonstrates)*, **will it work?**

CHILDREN: Yes!

CLOWN: *(Puts bulb in lamp. Clicks lamp switch on and off. Bulb doesn't light.)* **It's not working. Hmmm.** *(CLOWN walks around lamp.)* **Aah! It's not plugged in. There's no power.** *(CLOWN picks up extension cord. Safety tip follows.)* **How many have an extension cord at home? ... See these metal prongs? ... You mustn't ever touch the prongs when you're plugging them into electricity. Uncontrolled power is dangerous.** *(Plugs lamp into extension cord.)* **Now let's see what happens.** *(Clicks lamp switch on and off. Bulb doesn't light. CLOWN looks puzzled.)* **Whatever is the matter?**

CHILDREN: It's not plugged into the wall!

CLOWN: *(Reacts.)* **Oh, no! Not plugged into the wall! I'll take care of that.** *(Plugs extension cord into wall. Bulb lights.)* **Wheee! Let's give the light bulb a hand!** *(Everyone claps. Note: Happy-Go-Litely says that periodic breaks of this nature increase children's attention span.)* **Let's talk about the bulb. When it is connected to power, the wire heats and the bulb gives light. Right?**

*Performance rights for this skit are granted with the purchase of this book. No further permission is needed to adapt or integrate this skit within any performance situation for clown ministry.

CHILDREN: Right!

CLOWN: Let's talk about our hearts. We need power in our lives in order to live happily in Jesus. The name of this power is the "Holy Spirit." It is another name for Jesus, who comes to live in our hearts. Just as the bulb needed power to light it, we need Jesus to light our hearts. He has told us to "let our light shine." What is our "light?" *(CLOWN prompts the correct answer.)*

It is the love that Jesus feels for us. He wants us to show it to every boy and girl. How do we do that? By the way we live and love. *(CLOWN picks up Easter basket and puts it upside down over light.)* **What happens if we hide the light?**

CHILDREN: It gets dark!

CLOWN: Can anybody see it?

CHILDREN: No!

CLOWN: Exactly. Let's make sure that none of our friends is left in the dark. *(Removes basket from lamp.)* **Let's tell them about Jesus and his power to keep us happy eternally.**

Prayer*

(Prayer is conducted in "repeat after me" style and in words that children readily understand. No "preacher-ese" spoken here! Happy-Go-Litely leads, and the children follow, one phrase at a time. Here is a typical children's prayer:)

Lord Jesus, . . . I love you . . . and I'm so glad you love me. . . . You loved me when I was wrong and disobeyed you . . .for that's what sin is . . . disobeying God. . . . And we know that no sin will enter into heaven. . . . Jesus, you showed your love to me . . . by dying for my sins on the cross . . . so my sins would be forgiven. . . . I thank you for that. . . . I love you and want you to be my very best friend. . . . I ask you to come and live in my heart . . . to forgive and take away every sin . . .

*Performance rights for this prayer are granted with the purchase of this book. No further permission is needed to adapt or integrate this prayer within any performance situation for clown ministry.

and to change my life. ... You died for me. ... I promise, with your help, to live for you ... every single day. ... I will share your love ... read your word (the Bible) ... and talk to you in prayer as my friend ... every single day. ... Thank you, Jesus, for loving me and forgiving me ... and for being my very best friend. ... In Jesus' name ... Amen!

Happy-Go-Litely with his son, Joshua

Simon ministers to a group of children

Simon

Micah

RANDOLPH J. CHRISTENSEN

The Reverend Randolph J. Christensen once said that there was no way in the world that he would appear in a clown costume. Funny thing, he now has *two* clown persons — Micah and Simon! Randy's first experience with clowning was at a children's hospital. He prayed, "Lord, if you really want me to do this, you will have to give me a burden for kids." He got the burden. Since then, he has directed the North Central Bible College Clown Team and the Children's Ministry Department, has traveled full time, directing the "Celebration Express" (a children's ministry team), and has served as children's pastor at two churches. He is currently the children's and evangelism pastor at First Assembly of God Christian Center in Sioux Falls, South Dakota. Using puppetry and magic, Randy ministers in hospitals, at parties, children's church services, camps, picnics and school assemblies. He also teaches annually at the Fellowship of Christian Magicians' National Convention. All of this came about because a college roommate convinced him to "try it just once."

Randy says, "Obviously, God has given me the burden to see children come to him. I praise him for that!"

Randy ministers as a speaking clown, approaching clowning as a traditional art for reaching and teaching people.

"I see it as a great ministry," he says, "but don't agree with the total concept of 'Christ, the clown.' I teach that clowns carry many parallels with Christ (his compassion, etc.), but I don't go a lot further. Also, I think that Christian clowns can get so involved in symbolism that they are way over some people's heads. Clowns should simply be clowns . . . and touch people's hurts and hearts."

The following skit is one that Randy wrote as a tool for teaching about priorities.

The Ladder of Life*

AIM: to help children understand the importance of good priorities

THEME: If a person places Christ first in his life, he will have a solid Christian life.

SCRIPTURE: Matthew 6:33 and 22:37; Luke 6:47-48

CHARACTERS: RANDEE (straight person or whiteface)
JOEY (silent clown)

PROPS: a six-foot ladder, five signs (Each has one word on it. The words are: *JESUS, CHURCH, FRIENDS, CIRCUS, PUPPY.*)

RANDEE: *(Addresses audience.)* **It's sure good to see all of you here today! We're going to have an exciting —**

JOEY: *(Enters, carrying ladder and signs. Crosses in front of RANDEE.)*

RANDEE: Hey! Hey! What are you doing?

JOEY: *(Sets up the ladder and prepares to climb it.)*

*Performance rights for this skit are granted with the purchase of this book. No further permission is needed to adapt or integrate this skit within any performance situation for clown ministry.

RANDEE: Joey! What happened? Did a light bulb burn out?

JOEY: *(Shakes his head* no.*)*

RANDEE: Then what are you doing?

JOEY: *(Points at the ladder, then points at self.)*

RANDEE: You mean it's your ladder?

JOEY: *(Shakes his head* no. *He again points to the ladder, then to himself. With a finger, he traces a heart on his chest.)*

RANDEE: Ohhhh . . . a heart. I understand now. You love your ladder.

JOEY: *(Shakes his head* no *again. He pantomimes* life *by putting his hand on his heart and pulling his hand dramatically away.)*

RANDEE: Your life. . . . Your life?

JOEY: *(Nods his head* yes.*)*

RANDEE: That's your "ladder of life!"

JOEY: *(Excitedly nods his head* yes.*)*

RANDEE: A ladder of life? What's that?

JOEY: *(Hands the signs to RANDEE.)*

RANDEE: What are these? Oh, I see. *(RANDEE holds up the first sign,* PUPPY.*)* **Puppy. . . . I bet you really love your puppy, don't you, Joey?**

JOEY: *(Nods* yes, *and pats his heart.)*

RANDEE: Well, let's put this up here somewhere.

JOEY: *(Takes the* PUPPY *sign and places it on the side of the top rung so that all can see it.)*

RANDEE: You must really love your puppy to put it at the top of your ladder! What's next here? *(RANDEE and JOEY continue going through the signs, placing them on the ladder in the following order from top to bottom:* PUPPY, FRIENDS, JESUS, CIRCUS, CHURCH.*)*

JOEY: *(Once the signs are in place, JOEY begins to climb the ladder. The ladder wobbles.)*

RANDEE: Be careful, Joey. That doesn't look very solid!

JOEY: *(He is almost to the top, and begins to fall.)*

RANDEE: Watch out!!!

JOEY: *(Falls backward off the ladder. He lands on his feet and allows his body to continue backward. RANDEE catches him under his arms, absorbing the impact of the fall, and JOEY never really loses his balance.)*

RANDEE: *(Lifts JOEY to a standing position. Note: Lift with legs* *to avoid back strain.)* **Are you OK, Joey?**

JOEY: *(Shaking, JOEY nods* yes.*)*

RANDEE: I think I know what's wrong here. Joey, your ladder of life is all out of order. You need to move a few of these things around if you want to have a sturdy life. Now, at the top, you have "puppy." Do you think that your puppy is more important than your friends?

JOEY: *(Excitedly nods his head* yes.*)*

RANDEE: Do you really think so?

JOEY: *(Stops and thinks for a moment, then shakes his head* no. *RANDEE and JOEY rearrange the signs until they are in the following order from top to bottom:* JESUS, CHURCH, FRIENDS, PUPPY, CIRCUS.*)*

RANDEE: There! That looks much sturdier, doesn't it?

JOEY: *(Climbs to the top of the ladder.)*

RANDEE: *(Addressing the audience)* **You see, when a person has Christ at the top, as number one in his life, he will have a sturdy life that won't fall all apart. Now . . .** *(He looks up at JOEY.)* **Joey, aren't you going to come down?**

JOEY: *(Shakes his head* no *and looks frightened.)*

RANDEE: Oh, Joey, are you scared?

JOEY: *(Nods his head* yes.*)*

RANDEE: That's all right, Joey. I'll help you down. *(RANDEE puts his hand up to help JOEY, while looking at the audience.)*

JOEY: *(Climbs down the ladder, and instead of taking RANDEE'S hand, he puts his hand on RANDEE'S head, using it as a brace.)*

RANDEE: Joey! Oh, well, that's all right. I guess that's what friends are for . . . leaning on. Now remember, keep Jesus as number one in your life, Joey.

JOEY: *(Happily nods* yes, *picks up his ladder, and exits.)*

RANDEE: Goodbye, Joey. *(RANDEE may then further address the audience or exit.)*

MARCIA GRAHAM
Popcorn
(photo by Leslie Homann)

Marcia Graham ("Popcorn") is currently the coordinator of Lysander-VanBuren Youth Services in Upstate New York. She has an appropriate background for playing the role of a clown: Marcia grew up in the theater and trained for many years in drama and dance. Among her professional credits is a two-year position emceeing local television segments of the nationally syndicated Mickey Mouse Club show. She also moved into the church arena, acting with the Church Row Players, an ecumenical group in the Washington, D.C., area.

Nine years ago, Popcorn was born as Marcia's colorful clown person, who performs both professionally and as a Christian clown. Popcorn really gets around. She has even entertained at the White House for Mrs. Reagan and the Foster Grandparents Program.

Marcia also leads workshops and seminars on clowning, clown ministry and Christian clown scripting. "The Bible According to Popcorn" (printed on the following pages) is one of her scripts. Says Marcia:

"A friend of mine suggested 'mixed-up Bible stories' to me awhile back (though she gives the credit to the television cartoon character Bullwinkle). She told me that as a clown storyteller, she sometimes told fairy tales wrong and allowed the children to correct her. Not only did this sort of clowning go well with her characterization of a bumbling, sweet-hearted clown, it also empowered her small listeners to feel that they had something to teach and to share.

I decided to adapt the technique for clown ministry with younger children."

Marcia suggests that this kind of mixed-up script be kept short so that it doesn't become wearisome and lose its humor. "Even though it's obvious," she adds, "I'll mention it anyway: this will not work if your young audience is unfamiliar with biblical versions. It is best to stick with well-known stories."

The Bible According to Popcorn*

(Looking up) **What's that, Daddy God? You mean you want me to teach the lesson today? Really? Oh, boy!**

(To the kids) **Golly, gee whiz, I get to tell the story today. Let's see; where should I start? Oh, I know. You remember Moses? He was born in Bethlehem!** *(Big silly grin — so pleased with herself for telling this story. By this time, the kids are looking puzzled, and at least one child will say, "No, that's not right!")*

Nooo? Nooo? Well, then, who was it that was born in Bethlehem? *(The kids will say, "Jesus.")* **Oooh. . . . Hey, you guys are pretty smart! I remember now: Moses was the guy God gave the eight commandments to!** *(As the children say, "No," she does a double-take or an opening and closing of her mouth as a double-take, as if to signify puzzlement and, "You mean I didn't get it right again?".)*

***Ten* commandments, you say? You don't say! Well, let's see. Maybe we'd better go back to the beginning. . . . In the beginning, God created Levi's and Nike's . . .** *(Now the kids are really hollering it up.)* **He didn't? . . . Well, what did he create?** *(She stops, and the children let her know what God created.)*

Gee, God did all that? Wow! He's some God, isn't he? . . . He sure made you kids smart. Now, let's see. Let me try again. . . . *(Pauses to think for a second.)* **Remember Abraham? . . . Well, God told him,** *(Walking closer to the children, speaking in a lower, conspiratorial voice)* **"Abraham, I want you to build an ark, 'cause it's going to rain for 40 days and 40 nights!" So Abraham went down to the lumberyard . . .** *(She keeps up this*

*Reprinted with permission from *Laugh-Makers, The Magazine for Family Entertainers,* P.O. Box 160, Syracuse, New York 13215.

patter long enough for the kids to shout her down.) **What's wrong?**

Nooo?! ... *(Disbelief)* **Noah? ... Really? Boy, you sure Know-ah lot! So it was Noah, huh, who God asked to bring two-by-two on the ark all the plants and flowers and trees ... ?** *(Looking confused with a "What are they hollering about?" expression, she asks:)* **Well, what *did* he bring on the ark?** *(Again, she stops to go over the kinds of animals.)*

Speaking of animals ... do you remember Daniel? He was thrown into the nasty ol' koala bear's den. ... Well, what *was* in the den? *(If you're working with another clown, he might pipe up and say, "The TV.")*

My, oh, my, I guess I need to go back and study some more, don't I? ... You kids were wonderful. ... *(Looking up)* **Aren't they wonderful, Daddy God?!**

THE ST. MARGARET'S MERRY CLOWN TROUPE

Connie Geiss is youth minister at St. Margaret Mary Parish in Algonquin, Illinois. Her group, "The St. Margaret's Merry Clown Troupe," is made up of high school-age young people and, says Connie, "their not-so-young adult coordinators and coworkers." The troupe was formed in 1982 by Father Stephen Potter, associate pastor, and Connie. She explains, "Since that time, St. Margaret's Merry Clowns have visited nursing homes, hospitals, zoos, parties and institutions for the handicapped. They have taken part in retreats, religious education classes, worship services — anywhere their love, joy and compassion can be shared. This special ministry has provided tremendous opportunities for growth and healing, for the clowns as well as for the recipients of the clowns' message."

The following skit was one they wrote and used as a farewell for their associate pastor, but it could be effective in other settings.

Friendship — A Circle of Love*

CAST: 11 clowns

PROPS: jumprope, umbrella (children's or brightly decorated), feather dusters, wagon or wheelbarrow (decorated with balloons, streamers, etc.), helium balloon, love balloon

SCENE: Clowns are involved in various activities. CLOWNS 1 and 2 are jumping rope; CLOWNS 3, 4 and 5 are playing leapfrog, while CLOWN 6 is sitting at one side (lonely). CLOWN 7 is walking tightrope (on floor) in trembling and frightened manner; and CLOWNS 8 and 9 are fighting (mimed boxing or sword fight with feather dusters).

CLOWN 6: *(Rises. Moves to Center to speak. Other clowns freeze activity.)* **"Some people come into our lives and quickly go. Others stay for a while, leave footprints on our hearts, and we are never quite the same again."** *(Anonymous quote. Activity resumes, and CLOWN 6 returns to position.)*

CLOWN 7: *(While trying to balance, mimes tightrope-walking to Center and speaks. Again, activity freezes.)* **But, as we all know, that's easier said than done. It's pretty risky! It's not safe at all!**

(Activity resumes. Enter FATHER CLOWN, pulling a wagon or pushing a wheelbarrow containing NEW CLOWN, who looks apprehensive and overwhelmed. FATHER CLOWN

*Performance rights for this skit are granted with the purchase of this book. No further permission is needed to adapt or integrate this skit within any performance situation for clown ministry.

encourages NEW CLOWN to get out; demands that she get out; and finally, lifts her out and drives off.

NEW CLOWN is shy and frightened as CLOWNS 3, 4 and 5 come to "inspect" her. Then she tries to act brave — sticks out chest and struts around. As CLOWNS 3, 4 and 5 begin to welcome her, she relaxes, looks relieved, and allows herself to be drawn into the game of leapfrog — with reservations.

After second round of leapfrog, NEW CLOWN summersaults or trips off to side and lands next to CLOWN 6. She tries to cheer up CLOWN 6, who resists at first, but also gets drawn into the game of leapfrog. CLOWN 6 is made to feel welcome and part of group, too.

NEW CLOWN notices CLOWN 7, who is trembling at the prospect of having to walk the rope. He can't catch his balance. NEW CLOWN excitedly mimes trying to catch him, and then gets an idea. She takes helium balloon and ties it to back of CLOWN 7's belt. CLOWN 7 confidently and exuberantly crosses the tightrope.)

CLOWN 1: *(Walks Center. Activity freezes.)* **The new clown was beginning to feel pretty happy. She was making friends and liked being able to help people. So, when she saw the two little clowns fighting, she remembered the scripture, "Blessed are the peacemakers."**

(Activity resumes. NEW CLOWN is walking along, whistling in mime, as if she has not a care in the world, when she notices the two clowns fighting. She rushes over to break up their fight. The two stop momentarily, and NEW CLOWN gets socked in the eye. She reels away and mouths to audience, "Blessed are the peacemakers?".

She goes off to think for a moment, then reaches into pocket and pulls out a love balloon. Offers it to one of the fighting clowns; encourages him to play catch with his adversary. After some resistance, they begin playing with balloon.

CLOWN 4 is miming a leapfrog up to grab an apple off a tree; is determined, but is getting discouraged. NEW CLOWN offers to help — grabs her from behind, around waist. They both jump, but still can't reach the apple. NEW CLOWN thinks, then goes off to side to pray, arms open toward heaven. Other clowns, without seeming to know why, come Downstage to form a pyramid.

CLOWN 4 climbs up, gets apple, and shares it with the group.)

CLOWN 8: *(Comes Center. Activity freezes.)* **The new clown had known she was to play with her new friends just a short time, but when the father clown returned for her, she was sad; her friends were sad, too, and a little angry.**

(FATHER CLOWN returns with wagon as activity resumes. Clowns mime various angry and sad reactions. Some cry. CLOWNS 8 and 9 threaten FATHER CLOWN with their feather dusters.

NEW CLOWN goes to each clown or clown group and tentatively and gently makes contact — often through miming previous interchange; i.e., fighting, tightrope-walking, etc. As contact is made, NEW CLOWN leads each clown to Center to form one group. NEW CLOWN joins their hands. When all clowns are together, they end by singing a song about friendship. NEW CLOWN leaves with FATHER CLOWN during song.)

CLOWN 6: "Some people come into our lives and quickly go. Some stay for a while, leave footprints on our hearts, and we are never quite the same again."

RUTH HANSEN
Salty

Ruth Hansen is founder of "The Christian Clowns," a Michigan group that has been in existence for many years. She is a gifted teacher and workshop leader who presents approximately 25 Christian Clowning worship services and/or programs yearly for churches of all denominations. She is also a veteran theatrical director, producer, and actress, a mother, and a grandmother.

Ruth says, "God has given me wonderful opportunities to combine my love and knowledge of theater with this unique art form (clowning)."

The following is one of her original skits:

Where Your Heart Is*

CAST: Two fun-loving clowns, a reader

PROPS: Baby blanket, manger (approximately 1½' x 8" x 6"), a three-legged stool

SUGGESTED BACKGROUND MUSIC: "Somewhere Over the Rainbow," "Jesus Loves the Little Children," "Happiness Is the Lord," "Into My Heart," "It Is No Secret," and "melodrama music" (or, grasp two octaves on the piano and "shake" thumbs and fifth fingers back and forth on the keys), "I Believe in Miracles," "Amazing Grace," "I Surrender All," "I Have Decided to Follow Jesus"

MUSIC: "Somewhere Over the Rainbow"

READER: Once upon time in a land not far from here there lived a happy clown who owned a beautiful blanket.

NO. 1: *(Enter down center aisle, drag blanket behind, clenched tightly in right fist. Grin, nod right, left, at congregation. Halfway down, stop, pull blanket to left shoulder. Cross left arm over blanket, hug it. Move shoulders right and left, rocking. Slowly turn completely around. Move Center Front.)*

READER: The clown loved the blanket very much, because he/she could pretend to be so many funny and different people. The blanket was like a good friend.

MUSIC: "Jesus Loves the Little Children"

NO. 1: *(Place blanket over head, peek out, laugh. Pull blanket off face, tie under chin, fold hands under chin, purse lips, move shoulders right and left. Grin. Pull blanket down, tie around waist.*

*Performance rights for this skit are granted with the purchase of this book. No further permission is needed to adapt or integrate this skit within any performance situation for clown ministry.

Grin, slap right knee with right hand. Throw both hands palms up, waist high. Make into fists. Grin, wiggle all over.)

READER: In fact, this blanket was his/her most prized possession and he/she could never get along without it.

NO. 1: *(Move right of altar area. Sit on stool, face full front. Cross legs in front, hug blanket to chest. Grin, rock slightly.)*

READER: But one day into this land came a Christian.

MUSIC: "Happiness Is the Lord"

NO. 2: *(Enter down center aisle slowly, carrying manger in both hands, chest high. Present manger while entering.)*

MUSIC: "Into My Heart"

NO. 1: *(Stop rocking, watch NO. 2. Keep eyes on manger.)*

NO. 2: *(Present manger, God. Slowly lower manger, place right side on altar. Turn, see NO. 1. Grin. Move right of NO. 1. Extend left hand to blanket.)*

MUSIC: "It Is No Secret"

NO. 2: *(Step back with right foot, point to blanket with left hand index finger, move to right of manger, point at manger with right hand index finger.)*

NO. 1: *(Watch NO. 2's finger. Drop mouth open, wrinkle brow, stick out chin. Blank look on face.)*

NO. 2: *(Repeat action as before twice. Faster each time.)*

NO. 1: *(Jump up, look at congregation, mouth and eyes wide open. Clutch blanket to chest, stretch both hands, with blanket out to manger. Look at NO. 2.)*

NO. 2: *(Grin, look at congregation, shake head "yes." Grab end of blanket.)*

NO. 1: *(Clutch blanket back to chest, shake head "no.")*

NO. 2: *(Look at congregation, back at NO. 1, shake head "Yes.")*

MUSIC: Melodrama music.

NO. 1 & NO. 2: *(Tug back and forth 3 times.)*

NO. 1: *(Pull loose, run down right, turn back to NO. 2. Hug blanket to self, bury face in blanket. Shake all over.*

NO. 2: *[Surprised] (Shrug shoulders. Move left of altar, kneel, fold hands, bow head.)*

MUSIC: "I Believe in Miracles"

NO. 1: *(Slowly turn head toward congregation. Slowly look at NO. 2. Move toward NO. 2, still clutching blanket to chest.)*

NO. 2: *(Rise. Smile gently at NO. 1. Bring both arms out waist high* *toward blanket, slowly swing both arms toward manger. Move right arm low, left arm above [don't block view of manger], freeze.)*

NO. 1: *(Move left of altar, kneel. Hold blanket between hands, hanging down. Look at NO. 2.)*

MUSIC: "Amazing Grace"

NO. 2: *(Turn toward congregation at waist. Extend arms, palms up, face full front. Turn head right, swing right arm back, extend out shoulder high. Repeat with left arm. Turn head center, bend head back, look straight up. Keep legs and knees together. Hang head, shoulders straight. Turn palms down, with one sweeping motion, swing arms down, cross each other, continue until arms are extended above head, palms face in. At same time, bring head down to chest, slowly raise face full front, big smile.)*

READER: The spirit of God descended upon Jesus like a dove, and a voice from heaven said, "This is my beloved son in whom I am well pleased." *(Matthew 3:17b)*

MUSIC: "I Surrender All"

NO. 2: *(Bring arms down, palms up, elbows waist high. Extend both hands to blanket, swing arms to manger, smile.)*

NO. 1: *(Look at congregation, smile. Stand. Present blanket, God. Look at congregation, take deep breath. Look at NO. 2.)*

NO. 2: *(Grin, shake head "yes.")*

NO. 1: *(Move to left of manger. Lay blanket in manger, arrange neatly. Take 2 steps back. Move forward, slowly reach for blanket with right hand.)*

MUSIC: "I Have Decided to Follow Jesus"

NO. 2: *(Extend left hand. Gently take NO. 1's hand and smile.)*

NO. 1: *(Grin at congregation, take deep breath.)*

NO. 1 & NO. 2: *(Exit down center aisle.)*

READER: Hear the words of Jesus. "Do not lay up for yourself treasures on earth, where moth and rust consume and where thieves break in and steal. But lay up for yourself treasures in heaven, where neither moth nor rust consumes and where thieves do not break in and steal. For where your treasure is, there will your heart be also." *(Have prayer)*

BARBARA H. VANDER HAAR and ELLEN A. LUDWIG

Sparky and Gus

Barbara and Ellen are friends who enjoy working together — writing their own skits and performing clown acts for senior citizens, church groups, and Christian schools. They spend many hours writing and rewriting, then many more hours practicing each action and facial expression until they are satisfied with every aspect of their performance. Barbara says, "When our message moves someone to laughter or tears, we know our efforts were fruitful!"

Barbara has a degree in English Education from the University of Delaware and, for a while, taught sixth grade Language Arts. She is now a homemaker, free-lance writer, clown performer, and puppeteer. She is Orthodox Presbyterian.

Ellen became interested in drama while working toward a secretarial degree at the University of Delaware. She is a full-time secretary and a part-time clown minister. Ellen is Baptist.

Here are some valuable pointers that "Sparky" and "Gus" would like to share:

1. Look professional. Use good quality clown make-up and brushes.

2. Practice, practice, practice! Ask someone to watch you practice and critique your act.

3. Use music to help you set moods. We have found that music contributes at least 50% to the mood you are trying to establish. (You don't need live music; taped music is fine.)

4. Time facial expressions and actions to music.

5. Additional note on music — You do not need to use music throughout your entire skit. You can use it to highlight very dramatic or emotional scenes.

6. Use simple props. You will thank yourself as you move them from place to place! Remember that elaborate props do not make your act, but practice and a professional attitude will!

The following skit was written by Barbara:

Clean Shirt, Clean Heart*

CAST: A tramp or shabbily dressed Auguste; a preacher clown

PROPS: 2 large tee shirts (1 clean and 1 dirty — see illustration); powerful flashlight and duct tape; Bible; 3 empty laundry detergent boxes (see illustration); play money (coins & bills); hammer; pail or plastic dishpan; sign that says, "Laundromat" (mount on wall over detergent boxes); 3 large sheets of paper folded, with directions written on each (see illustration). Place directions inside each box as illustration directs.

Tramp enters from the rear, obviously distraught. He is wearing tattered but clean clothes with dirty tee shirt worn over everything else. He cries, looks down at his shirt, then

*Performance rights for this skit are granted with the purchase of this book. No further permission is needed to adapt or integrate this skit within any performance situation for clown ministry.

holds his nose. He clearly does not know what to do with his dirty, smelly tee shirt. He can interact with the audience on his way.

As he approaches the front of the stage area, he spies a laundromat! He brightens; this is just what he's been looking for! Eagerly, he runs to the laundromat sign and inspects the first detergent box.

It is labeled "MONEY FLAKES." He picks it up, carefully holding it so that the audience can also read the label. He shakes the box; it rattles! Then he reaches inside and pulls out directions that read, "Wallow in it." Scratching his head, he wonders how he is supposed to do that! Then, as an idea occurs to him, he turns the box up-side-down and shakes the money all over the floor. The money scatters and bounces everywhere. Grinning widely, he gets down on the floor and rolls around gleefully in the money.

After jumping up quickly, he prances around the stage, *assuming* that his shirt is clean. He glances down and is horrified to discover that it is still dirty! With growing agitation, he runs around the stage looking for more detergent. In his haste, he trips over the second box. He quickly recovers and picks up the box. It is labeled "POWER POWDER." Reaching inside, he pulls out directions that say, "Pound it out." He removes a hammer from inside the box.

Just as he is getting ready to pound his shirt with the hammer, he remembers something quite urgent. He is still wearing the shirt! Chuckling with embarrassment, he removes his tee shirt and places it on the floor. *(Remember to put something under the shirt before pounding so that you will not damage the floor.)* **He then proceeds to hammer away enthusiastically on the shirt. He finishes, then holds the shirt up to examine it. Oh, no! The shirt is still dirty! After a moment of angry silence, he balls up the shirt and throws it on the floor in contempt.**

Extremely frustrated, he puts his head in his hands and starts to cry. *(Dim the lights.)* **He cries and cries pathetically, getting louder until he is howling. Finally, the preacher clown enters. Hearing the wails of Tramp, he goes to him and touches his shoulder. Tramp looks up, still sobbing loudly.**

Preacher tries to comfort him by kneeling beside him and putting his arm around Tramp. Finally, Tramp snorts once or twice, blows his nose loudly, then grows quiet.

Lovingly, Preacher offers his hand and helps Tramp stand. He then pulls out a plastic dishpan and another detergent box. *(These should be hidden until now.)* **He turns the detergent box so that the audience and Tramp can read it. "JESUS" is written on it, and underneath it says, "No Additives."** *(See illustration.)*

Tramp scoffs at this idea, indicating the other two detergents that did not work. Why should this one be any better? Preacher is persistent and holds out hand to receive Tramp's dirty shirt. Tramp shrugs, picks up shirt, and hands it to Preacher.

Preacher drops the shirt into the dishpan and opens the new detergent box. He pulls out the directions and holds them for Tramp to read. They say, "WASH IT AWAY."

Half-heartedly, Tramp takes the box and turns it upside-down to pour the contents on the shirt. *(As he turns it, he should discreetly turn on the flashlight that is taped inside the box.)* **To his amazement, it appears that light is pouring out of the box! He "pours it on." He sets the box down, with the light still visible, then proceeds to "wash" his shirt.**

After a very brief time, Tramp removes his shirt *(The clean one)* **from the dishpan and holds it up for everyone to see.** *(Make sure the dirty shirt is hidden from audience's view. Bring lights up.)* **He is truly surprised and excited. Vigorously, he embraces Preacher, then runs through the audience dancing and jumping in his delirious excitement! After a short time, he puts on his VERY CLEAN shirt, prances around some more, kicks up heels, and exits. Preacher follows him out, showing the audience that the back of Tramp's shirt says, "Forgiven."**

NOTE: Try to keep the back of the clean shirt hidden from the audience until Tramp exits. It will make a lasting impression on them if they see "Forgiven" written boldly on TRAMP's back as he leaves the room.

Front

Back

Stained Shirt
(Tramp enters with this on.)

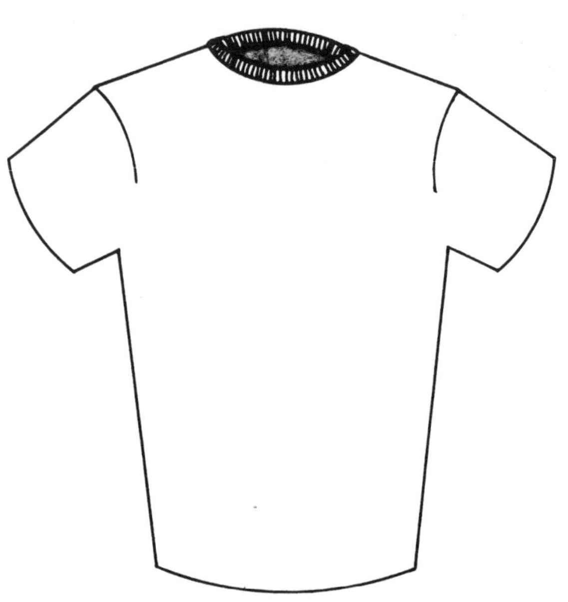

Front

Back

Clean Shirt
(Tramp exits with this shirt.)

Box 3

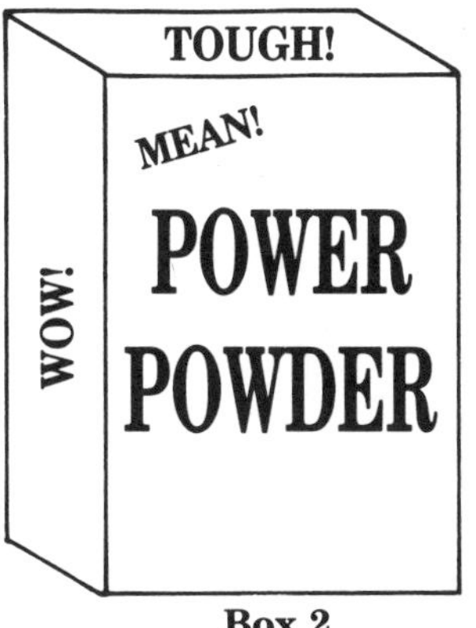

Box 2

Box 1

1. Use empty detergent boxes (large.)
2. Cover them with brown paper. Cover "Jesus" box in white.
3. Label them with a black marker.
4. Put play money in "Box 1."
5. Put hammer in second box.
6. Tape flashlight securely in third box.

Directions inside boxes

WASH IT AWAY	POUND IT OUT!!!	WALLOW IN IT!!!
Box 3	Box 2	Box 1

RESOURCES

BOOKS

Burgess, Hovey. *Circus Techniques.* Brian Dube Inc., New York, rev. ed., 1990.

Feder, Happy Jack. *Clown Skits for Everyone.* Meriwether Publishing Ltd., Colorado Springs, CO, second edition, 1991. Everything you need to know to become a performing clown.

Feder, Happy Jack. *Mime Time.* Meriwether Publishing Ltd., Colorado Springs, CO, second edition, 1992. A "how to" manual for beginning mimes with make-up, prop and staging techniques.

Fife, Bruce, et al. *Creative Clowning.* Piccadilly Books, Colorado Springs, CO, second edition, 1992.

Hartisch, Karl, "Whitey." *Introduction to Clowning.* Available from: Clowns of America, P.O. Box 570, Lake Jackson, TX 77566.

Kerns, Ernie. *How to Be a Magic Clown.* 2 vols. Magic, Inc., Chicago, IL, 1960, 1968.

Kipnis, Claude. *The Mime Book.* Meriwether Publishing Ltd., Colorado Springs, CO, second edition, 1988. A comprehensive guide to the art of mime.

Litherland, Janet. *Everything New and Who's Who in Clown Ministry.* Meriwether Publishing Ltd., Colorado Springs, CO, 1993. Advanced clown ministry text including seventy-five skits for special days.

McVicar, Wes. *Clown Act Omnibus.* Meriwether Publishing Ltd., Colorado Springs, CO, second edition, 1987. Includes over 200 workable clown acts (secular).

Stolzenberg, Mark. *Be a Clown.* Sterling Publishing Co., New York, NY, 1989.

Toomey, Susie Kelly. *Mime Ministry.* Meriwether Publishing Ltd., Colorado Springs, CO, 1987. The first complete guidebook on Christian mime.

Wiley, Jack. *Basic Circus Skills.* Solipaz Publishing Co., Lodi, CA, third edition, 1990.

CATALOGS

Clown, Mime, Puppet, Dance, Drama & Storytelling Resources Catalog. Published once a year. Available from Contemporary Drama Service, Box 7710, Colorado Springs, CO 80933.

FILMS

From Mass Media Ministries, 2116 N. Charles St., Baltimore, MD 21218:

A Clown Is Born

The Mark of a Clown

That's Life

Available from most denominational media centers:

The Parable. Council of Churches of New York City.

ORGANIZATIONS

Clown Camp, University of Wisconsin La Crosse, 1725 State Street, La Crosse, WI 54601.

The Clown Hall of Fame & Research Center, Inc., 114 North Third Street, Delavan, WI 53115.

Clowns of America International, P.O. Box 570, Lake Jackson, TX 77566.

Fellowship of Christian Magicians, P.O. Box 385, Connersville, IN 47331.

International Shrine Clown Association, P.O. Box 440, North Reading, MA 01864.

National Clown Arts Council, Inc., 240 Swimming River Road, Colts Neck, NJ 07722.

Phoenix Power & Light Company, Inc., P.O. Box 86, Pine Valley, NY 14872.

Ringling Bros. and Barnum & Bailey Circus, Clown College, P.O. Box 9, Vienna, VA 22183.

World Clown Association, 418 S. Sixth Street, Pekin, IL 61554.

PERIODICALS

The New Calliope Magazine. Clowns of America International, Inc., P.O. Box 570, Lake Jackson, TX 77566-0570.

Circus Report. Don Marcks, 525 Oak Street, El Cerrito, CA 94530.

Clown Alley. International Shrine Clown Association, P.O. Box 440, North Reading, MA 01864.

Clowning Around. World Clown Association, 418 South Sixth Street, Pekin, IL 61554.

Clown Town Crier. Clown Hall of Fame & Research Center, Inc., 114 North Third Street, Delavan, WI 53115.

Laugh-Makers. 108 Berwyn Ave., Syracuse, NY 13210.

On One Wheel. Unicycling Society of America, Inc., P.O. Box 40534, Redford, MI 48240.

Phoenix Rising. Phoenix Power & Light Company, Inc., P.O. Box 86, Pine Valley, NY 14872.

Three Ring News. Midwest Clown Association, Gene Lee, Editor, 235 South Summit Street, Whitewater, WI 53190.

SKITS, PLAYS & ROUTINES

Available from Contemporary Drama Service, P.O. Box 7710, Colorado Springs, CO 80933:

The Clown as Minister I, by Janet Litherland. 7 skits.

The Clown as Minister II, by Janet Litherland. 5 skits.

Clown Hits and Skits, by Richard Strelak and Marty Sherman. 20 skits. *Secular content; includes booklet, "How to Write Your Own Clown Skits."*

Clown Mimes for Christian Ministry I & II, by Susie Kelly Toomey. 8 thematic clown mime skits demonstrating Christian principles.

The Clown's Bible, by Paul H. Waters. 15 skits about biblical events.

The Clown's Christmas Party, by James Brock. 30-minute play.

Here Come the Clowns, by Clarice Moon, 20 skits. *Secular content.*

Scripture Skits for a Troupe of Clowns, by Janet Litherland. 10 skits.

Skits for Clown Ministry, by Elizabeth Wilkinson.

Starlight, by Barbara H. Vander Haar and Ellen Ludwig.

Where Are You God?, by Barbara H. Vander Haar.

Yesu, by David Suhs, Barbara Smith-Jang and Frances Townsend.

BIBLIOGRAPHY

Bishop, George. *The World of Clowns.* Los Angeles: Brooke House Publishers, 1976.

Fenner, Mildred Sandison and Wolcott Fenner. *The Circus, Lure and Legend.* Englewood Cliffs, NJ: Prentice-Hall, Inc., 1970.

Gaer, Joseph. *The Lore of the Old Testament.* Boston: Little, Brown and Company, 1951.

Geyer, Nancy and Shirley Noll. *Team-Building in Church Groups.* Valley Forge: Judson Press, 1970.

Holy Bible, The (King James Version). Cleveland and New York: The World Publishing Company.

Holy Bible, The (Revised Standard Version). Grand Rapids: Zondervan Bible Publishers, 1952, 1946 and 1971.

Hugill, Beryl. *Bring on the Clowns.* Seacaucus, NJ: Chartwell Books, Inc., 1980.

Hurston, Herbert and Donald Attwater, eds. *Butler's Lives of the Saints.* 4 vols. Westminster, MD: Christian Classics, 1956.

Kehl, Tim. "Getting Started in Clown Ministry," *Shoddy Pad.* Nashville: United Methodist Communications, 1978.

Kerns, Ernie. *How to Be a Magic Clown.* 2 vols. Chicago: Magic, Inc., 1960, 1968.

Liebig, Ernie. "Be a Clown," *Church Recreation Magazine,* Vol. IX, Number 2. Nashville: The Sunday School Board of the Southern Baptist Convention, January-February-March, 1979.

Liebig, Ernie and Jean. *Clowning Is —* . Bullard, TX: Happy Enterprises, 1980.

McVicar, Wes. *Clown Act Omnibus.* Colorado Springs, CO: Meriwether Publishing Ltd., 1986.

Shaffer, Floyd. *An Introduction to Clown Ministry* (filmstrip). Colorado Springs, CO: Meriwether Publishing Ltd.

Speaight, George. *The Book of Clowns.* New York: MacMillan Publishing Co., Inc., 1980.

Swortzell, Lowell. *Here Come the Clowns.* New York: The Viking Press, 1978.

Walker, Williston. *A History of the Christian Church.* New York: Charles Scribner's Sons, 1959.

ABOUT THE AUTHOR

Photo by Dickinson-Brouwer Photography

Janet Litherland is the author of several works reflecting the arts in ministry, including plays, monologs, mime skits, Readers Theatre scripts, and liturgical dance choreography. Her books include ***Absolutely Unforgettable Parties! The Complete Banner Handbook, Everything New and Who's Who in Clown Ministry***, and ***The Clown Ministry Handbook,*** a bestseller.

In addition to her freelance writing career, Janet works as an editorial associate for a Florida magazine. She and her husband, Jerry, have two grown sons.

ORDER FORM

MERIWETHER PUBLISHING LTD.
P.O. BOX 7710
COLORADO SPRINGS, CO 80933
TELEPHONE: (719) 594-4422

Please send me the following books:

________ **The Clown Ministry Handbook #CC-B163** **$10.95**
by Janet Litherland
The first and most complete text on the art of clown ministry

________ **Everything New and Who's Who in Clown Ministry #CC-B126** **$10.95**
by Janet Litherland
Profiles of clown ministers plus 75 skits for special days

________ **Storytelling From the Bible #CC-B145** **$10.95**
by Janet Litherland
The art of biblical storytelling

________ **The Complete Banner Handbook #CC-B172** **$13.95**
by Janet Litherland
A complete guide to banner design and construction

________ **Mime Ministry #CC-B198** **$10.95**
by Susie Kelly Toomey
The first complete guidebook to Christian mime

________ **Elegantly Frugal Costumes #CC-B125** **$10.95**
by Shirley Dearing
A do-it-yourself costume maker's guide

________ **Clown Act Omnibus #CC-B118** **$12.95**
by Wes McVicar
Everything you need to know about clowning

These and other fine Meriwether Publishing books are available at your local bookstore or direct from the publisher. Use the handy order form on this page.

NAME: ____________________

ORGANIZATION NAME: ____________________

ADDRESS: ____________________

CITY: __________ STATE: ______ ZIP: ______

PHONE: ____________________

❑ **Check Enclosed**
❑ **Visa or MasterCard #** ____________________

Signature: ____________________ *Expiration Date:* __________
(required for Visa/MasterCard orders)

COLORADO RESIDENTS: Please add 3% sales tax.
SHIPPING: Include $2.75 for the first book and 50¢ for each additional book ordered.

❑ *Please send me a copy of your complete catalog of books and plays.*

ORDER FORM

MERIWETHER PUBLISHING LTD.
P.O. BOX 7710
COLORADO SPRINGS, CO 80933
TELEPHONE: (719) 594-4422

Please send me the following books:

_______ **The Clown Ministry Handbook #CC-B163** **$10.95**
by Janet Litherland
The first and most complete text on the art of clown ministry

_______ **Everything New and Who's Who in Clown Ministry #CC-B126** **$10.95**
by Janet Litherland
Profiles of clown ministers plus 75 skits for special days

_______ **Storytelling From the Bible #CC-B145** **$10.95**
by Janet Litherland
The art of biblical storytelling

_______ **The Complete Banner Handbook #CC-B172** **$13.95**
by Janet Litherland
A complete guide to banner design and construction

_______ **Mime Ministry #CC-B198** **$10.95**
by Susie Kelly Toomey
The first complete guidebook to Christian mime

_______ **Elegantly Frugal Costumes #CC-B125** **$10.95**
by Shirley Dearing
A do-it-yourself costume maker's guide

_______ **Clown Act Omnibus #CC-B118** **$12.95**
by Wes McVicar
Everything you need to know about clowning

These and other fine Meriwether Publishing books are available at your local bookstore or direct from the publisher. Use the handy order form on this page.

NAME: ______________________________

ORGANIZATION NAME: ______________________________

ADDRESS: ______________________________

CITY: ______________ STATE: ________ ZIP: ________

PHONE: ______________________________

❑ **Check Enclosed**
❑ **Visa or MasterCard #** ______________________________

Signature: ______________________ *Expiration Date:* ____________

(required for Visa/MasterCard orders)

COLORADO RESIDENTS: Please add 3% sales tax.
SHIPPING: Include $2.75 for the first book and 50¢ for each additional book ordered.

❑ *Please send me a copy of your complete catalog of books and plays.*